America
Triumphs

Walker and Company's World War II Series

AMERICA GOES TO WAR: 1941
AMERICA FIGHTS THE TIDE: 1942
AMERICA ON THE ATTACK: 1943
AMERICA STORMS THE BEACHES: 1944

America
Triumphs
1945

John Devaney

Walker and Company
New York

This book is dedicated to Sergeant John (Jack) McGillicuddy, killed in action in Belgium in January 1945, and to the thousands of other men and women who gave their lives in 1945 fighting for the Four Freedoms.

Copyright © 1995 by John Devaney

First published in the United States of America in 1995 by Walker Publishing Company, Inc.

Published simultaneously in Canada by Thomas Allen & Son Canada, Limited, Markham, Ontario

Library of Congress Cataloging-in-Publication Data
Devaney, John.
America triumphs : 1945 / John Devaney.
p.   cm. — (Walker and Company's World War II series)
ISBN 0-8027-8328-7   ISBN 0-8027-8347-3 (lib. bdg.)
1. World War, 1939–1945 — Juvenile literature.   2. World War, 1939–1945 — United States — Juvenile literature.
[1. World War, 1939–1945.   2. World War, 1939–1945 — United States.]   I. Title.   II. Series: World War II series.
D743.7.D45   1994
940.53 — dc20   94-13255
CIP
AC

Printed in the United States of America

2   4   6   8   10   9   7   5   3   1

AUTHOR'S NOTE

This is the fifth and final book in a series that began when my friend, the writer George Sullivan, pointed out to me one day in 1990 that America would be paying a salute to the fiftieth anniversary of Pearl Harbor on December 7, 1991. It seemed to me that America should know more about all the fiftieth anniversaries of World War II. I suggested to Amy Shields, the editor of Walker and Company's young adult books, that we put together a series of books looking back at America's battles of World War II. Amy greeted the idea with enthusiasm, as did her associate, Jeanne Gardner. Their skills and perceptions were as important to me as the keyboard on which I tap out these words. Amy has since left Walker for a mother's joys, but Jeanne has shepherded all five of these books to daylight. To both goes my gratitude.

Emily Easton was Amy's successor at Walker and Company. I cannot thank enough both Emily and her associate, Mary Perrotta Rich, for their counsel and patience. Walker and Company's art department receives my thanks for making the books so attractive. A copy editor with an encyclopedic knowledge, Victoria Haire, has saved me from making scores of what would have been embarrassing errors. Finally, my sincere thanks to the late Sam Walker, and to Beth Walker and Ramsey Walker for all they have done for this series.

PROLOGUE

World War II can be divided into two parts:
(1) the spreading of the Axis tide from 1939 to late 1942; (2) the ebbing of the Axis tide from late 1942 to 1945.

1939–42: *The Spreading Axis Tide*

Germany's dictator, Adolf Hitler, had been demanding more land—"living space," he called it—for Germans during the 1930s. He thumbed his nose at France and England as he seized land along the French border. In 1938 he grabbed Austria and Czechoslovakia.

When German tanks rolled into Poland on September 1, 1939, however, Great Britain and France declared war. Hitler's tanks and armored cars shot swiftly through Poland. His screeching Stuka dive bombers slaughtered Polish troops fighting on horseback.

No one, not even the British and French armies, was ready for Hitler's *blitzkrieg* ("lightning war"). The Allied soldiers, crouched inside the concrete forts of the Maginot Line on the French-German border, watched helplessly while Poland fell.

In 1940 Hitler and his allies—they would include Italy, Bulgaria, Rumania, Hungary, and Finland—smashed into France. Hitler's Panzer ("armored") juggernauts raced around the Maginot Line. The French surrendered. Hitler's tanks trapped the British near Dunkirk on the beaches of the English Channel.

The war seemed to be over, Hitler triumphant. German commanders waited for an order to hammer the British armies to pieces. But Hitler hesitated—even he had been stunned by his overnight victories—and he hesitated too long. Hundreds of thousands of soaked and bedraggled British soldiers escaped to England.

Hitler sent waves of bombers to burn English cities. His submarines ringed the island, cutting off food and weapons coming from America. He planned to starve the bomb-shattered English, alone now against him, into surrender.

By early 1941 Hitler's Panzers had swept all across Europe from the English Channel in the west to the Polish-Soviet border in the east. His swastika floated from the Arctic Circle in the north to Africa in the south. There his Afrika Korps, commanded by Erwin ("The Desert Fox") Rommel, was pushing the British back toward the Suez Canal. If Hitler took the canal, he could grab the oil-rich fields of the Middle East. That oil would fuel Germany's factories, tanks, and planes. Europe's millions would be Hitler's slaves.

Only one nation in Europe—the Union of Soviet Socialist Republics (USSR)—had the military might to challenge Hitler. The Communist regime of the USSR was led by the stumpy Josef Stalin. For years Hitler had sworn to destroy "Jewish Bolsheviks and Communists." Jewish Communists, he raved, had "stabbed Germany in the back" in World War I. His Gestapo secret police had herded millions of Jews, Communists, and other "racially inferior undesirables" into death camps such as Dachau and Buchenwald.

While busy overrunning Poland and France, however, Hitler had pretended to be friendly with Stalin, and had signed a peace agreement with the Soviets. But in 1941 Hitler decided to wipe out the threat of Stalin's Red Army while "cleansing the world of Russia's Jews and barbarians."

In June of 1941 Hitler's Panzers crashed into the Soviet Union. The surprised and poorly trained Red Army staggered backward. Near Christmas of 1941, German troops stood at the gates of Moscow. A Soviet surprise attack during a snowstorm drove them back.

That was Hitler's first defeat of the war. But the tide had not yet been halted.

In the United States, meanwhile, President Franklin Delano Roosevelt worried about Japan. The Japanese were eyeing the colonies of the

French, English, and Dutch in Southeast Asia. Japan needed the oil of Southeast Asia so that its navy and army, bigger than Hitler's, could overpower Asia. Japan and Germany were called the Axis powers. The two had set their sights on seizing half the globe.

Japan got about 80 percent of its oil from the United States. Roosevelt told Japan's leader, General Hideki Tojo: We are cutting off oil to Japan until you promise not to grab land that does not belong to you.

The Japanese leaders decided to go to war. On December 7, 1941, their carrier planes bombed the U.S. naval base at Pearl Harbor, killing more than 1,000 Americans.

Roosevelt met with England's leader, Winston Churchill. They formed what Roosevelt named a "United Nations" of more than twenty countries dedicated to defeating the Axis powers.

During the first five months of 1942 the Japanese swept westward to the borders of British-owned India. They drove southward to capture the U.S.-owned Philippines. On Bataan and Corregidor, near Manila, they captured more than 70,000 Americans and Filipinos. It was America's worst military defeat.

The Japanese also struck eastward across the vast Pacific. They hoisted their flag of the Rising Sun over islands more than 2,000 miles from Tokyo. Americans in San Francisco and Los Angeles stared nervously at the skies, expecting to see Japanese bombers overhead.

In New York City, sirens wailed to warn of German air raids that turned out to be false alarms. Schoolchildren were taught how to wear gas masks if the enemy dropped poison-gas bombs. They and their parents watched movies to learn how to spot enemy planes.

Late in 1942 Hitler's troops battled into the city of Stalingrad. If Hitler's armies held Stalingrad, they would cut off oil and food to the Soviet armies. When Stalingrad fell, Hitler exulted, his victory in Europe would be certain.

But the Axis tide—in Europe and in the Pacific—had rolled as far as it would roll.

LATE 1942–45: *The Ebbing Axis Tide*

As 250,000 Germans battled through the streets of Stalingrad, the Red Army threw a ring of tanks around the city. The German soldiers were trapped inside Stalingrad. Zero-degree winds whistled across their frozen faces. Early in 1943 the Germans surrendered. It was Hitler's worst defeat—and another was soon to come.

In November of 1942, an Allied army stormed ashore in North Africa. Commanded by General Dwight Eisenhower, American, Canadian, British, and Free French troops drove toward Tunisia. In Egypt, meanwhile, Rommel's Afrika Korps tanks had come to within a few hundred miles of the Suez Canal and Middle East oil. But at a place called El Alamein, Rommel's tanks ran out of gas. The British attacked; Rommel had to flee, racing back toward Tunisia. Hitler rushed some 200,000 troops to Tunisia and ordered Rommel to hold it against Eisenhower's armies. Eisenhower's American GIs and British Tommies hemmed in Rommel's army on Tunisian beaches. More than 250,000 German and Italian troops surrendered.

In 1943 Eisenhower's armies leapfrogged across the Mediterranean Sea, grabbing Sicily and landing in Italy. By the end of 1944 the Allied armies had fought their way north to capture the city of Rome.

In 1943 the Red Army pushed Hitler's armies back to where they had started in 1941. In 1944 the Soviet army rumbled westward into Bulgaria, Hungary, Rumania, and Poland. One by one, Hitler's allies surrendered.

On June 6, 1944, more than 100,000 Allied troops, commanded by Eisenhower, crossed a storm-tossed English Channel to land on the beaches of Normandy in France. The American Third Army, led by General George Patton, raced through a bombed-out hole in the German defenses and streaked toward Germany. Whipped on by Hitler, German generals formed a Siegfried Line that stopped Patton's tanks on the rim of Germany.

Near Christmas of 1944, more than 200,000 Germans surprised the Americans. Hidden by fog, German tanks smashed through the Ardennes Forest in Belgium and punched a huge bulge in the American-held line. American

American gunfire inflames a building inside a French town near St.-Lô. The St.-Lô break-through opened a wide pathway for General Patton's tanks to roll across France's flat plains toward Germany. *(Photo courtesy of the National Archives)*

paratroopers held off fierce attacks by the Germans, who had surrounded Bastogne, a town the Germans needed in order to widen the bulge. After more than a week of battling on snow-covered fields, American tanks broke through the German tanks battering Bastogne. The American fighting men had won what would be called the Battle of the Bulge. They had broken the back of Hitler's last offensive.

As 1945 began, Soviet guns thundered within a few hundred miles of Berlin. Thousands of American and British bombers dropped firebombs that turned German cities into flaming carpets.

The Japanese tide in the Pacific reached its farthest point in mid-1942 at Midway Island. American warships, outnumbered three to one, turned back a Japanese armada steaming toward Midway. The Japanese had planned to hop from Midway to seize Hawaii. Then their bombers could take off from Hawaii to bomb San Francisco and Los Angeles. Late in 1942 American marines landed on Guadalcanal Island in the South Pacific. They took it from the Japanese after months of bloody jungle battles.

In 1943 American warships drove across the Central Pacific, landing marines and soldiers on islands closer and closer to Japan. In 1944 Americans stormed onto the islands of Guam and Saipan. New B-29 Super Fortresses took off from Guam and Saipan to set fire to Japanese cities.

In the South Pacific, meanwhile, General Douglas MacArthur's American-Australian armies were pushing the Japanese backward on the 1,500-mile-long island of New Guinea, finally ending the Japanese threat to invade Australia. MacArthur's soldiers began an island-hopping drive toward the Philippines, from where MacArthur had escaped in 1942. His troops dodged around islands filled with Japanese to capture weakly held islands.

Late in 1944, MacArthur's troops waded

ashore on the Philippine island of Leyte. The
Japanese sent warships to blow away the troops
on Leyte's beaches. In the Battle of Leyte Gulf,
history's biggest naval battle, almost half of the
warships in Japan's battered Imperial Navy
were sunk.

The new year of 1945 dawned on Mac-
Arthur's 280,000 marines and soldiers boarding
ships to sail for the main Philippine island, Luzon, and the capital, Manila. Lying in wait on
Luzon were more than 250,000 Japanese—and a
deadly Japanese weapon.

Chapter One

JAN. 1: *Clark Field, near Manila, on the island of Luzon in the Philippines*

The twenty-three-year-old suicide pilot, Isao Matsuo, was writing to his parents. Within a few hours he and more than 100 other kamikaze pilots would climb into the cockpits and take off in planes loaded with explosives. They had sworn to give up their lives by crashing these kamikaze planes and themselves onto the decks of American warships and landing craft. The ships were carrying MacArthur's invasion army of 280,000 toward Luzon.

Kamikaze means "divine wind." Almost 500 years ago, an army of fierce Mongolian warriors had boarded ships and sailed across the Sea of Japan to attack the helpless Japanese. A typhoon blew away the invasion fleet. A "divine wind" had saved Japan, the Japanese believed. Now, a twentieth-century "divine wind"—brave men like Isao—might sink enough ships, Japanese admirals hoped, to again save Japan.

"Please congratulate me," Isao was writing to his parents. "I have been given a splendid opportunity to die. This is my last day before we begin our attacks on the American ships. The destiny of our homeland hinges on the decisive battle. . . . Then I shall fall like a blossom from a radiant cherry tree. May our deaths be as sudden and clean as the shattering of crystal."

A little later Isao and the other pilots walked toward their dive bombers.

"Do not be in too much of a hurry to die," an officer told Isao. "Choose a death which brings about the greatest number of American dead."

JAN. 1: *San Francisco, California*

A department store placed an ad in this morning's *Chronicle*. The ad pleaded with American workers to keep on turning out ships, guns, and planes to defeat the Axis powers.

"Hitler still has six million soldiers in the field," the ad said. "We are 2,000 miles from the Japanese mainland. Let's get first things done first before we dream about the gleaming postwar world and make any postwar plans."

JAN. 6: *Aboard the light cruiser* Columbia *off the island of Luzon, the Philippines*

Columbia's gunners crouched tensely in their turrets, scanning the sky for kamikazes. The time was a little past 5:00 P.M. as alarm bells clanged and sailors rushed to battle stations. A speck was skimming over the white-flecked waves—a speck whose yellow-tipped nose was aimed directly at the Gem.

Her crew called the *Columbia* "the Gem of the Ocean." Her white-frothed prow was leading a parade of more than 500 battleships, aircraft carriers, cruisers, destroyers, and minesweepers curving into Lingayen Gulf. They were shepherding more than 2,000 landing craft that would drop MacArthur's army of 280,000 onto Luzon's beaches. Their mission: to capture Manila, some 100 miles from the beaches.

The kamikazes had swooped down onto the invasion fleet for much of the past forty-eight hours. Dive bombers had crashed onto the decks of the cruisers *Louisville* and *Australia*, setting fires that killed twenty-six sailors and injured almost 100. Another slammed into the flight deck of the "baby" carrier *Manila Bay,* killing twenty-six and badly injuring fifty-six.

Columbia's gunners lobbed shells that blossomed white puffs of smoke in the sky. One dive bomber wiggled through the puffs. Its yellow-tipped nose, thought one gunner, was aiming straight for his bobbing Adam's apple. The gunner could see the yellow kamikaze bandanna tied around the pilot's head.

The gunner rose, panicky, and dived away from his turret. The kamikaze zoomed over the turret. Its whirling propeller missed the heads of sailors by inches. It cartwheeled across the deck and exploded, tearing open a jagged hole.

Its torpedo dropped through the hole, plunging two decks below. The torpedo blew up in a compartment where 500-pound shells were being hoisted up to *Columbia*'s guns.

The shells exploded, one after another. The *Columbia*'s decks heaved and shook as flames soared through the hole. Sailors dragged hoses toward fires above and below decks. The 300-degree heat blackened steel plates and scorched faces.

Within a half hour, the flames had been put out, but clouds of brown smoke and white steam floated above the Gem. She now carried thirteen dead and forty-four others with hands, faces, and chests badly burned.

JAN. 6: *Aboard the cruiser* Louisville *in Lingayen Gulf*

Rear Admiral Theodore Chandler's jaw tightened as the kamikaze—a Zeke to American gunners—swooped so low its wingtips brushed cables forty feet from where he stood on the bridge. Engine sputtering, the Zeke knifed into the bridge, spattering hunks of steel. Admiral Chandler flew backward, slamming into a gun turret. He rose groggily, his uniform soaked by gasoline spurting from the flaming Zeke. A sailor, pulling a fire hose, turned to see the admiral running toward him, a smoking torch. The sailor showered the admiral with foam that put out the fire. Medics hurried to the staggering admiral, his face and chest charred. They tried to help him to a first-aid station.

Chandler shook off the medics. He grabbed a hose and towed it to one of the dozen fires that now licked across the deck of the "Lady Lou." After a half hour, the fires were put out, the wrecked kamikaze and its dead pilot shoved into the sea.

Medics carried a gasping Admiral Chandler below. The flames had seared his lungs. Within hours he was dead, along with thirty-one of his crew. Another fifty-six were badly burned.

JAN. 6: *Invasion Fleet headquarters aboard the battleship* Pennsylvania *in Lingayen Gulf*

Admiral Elmer ("Oley") Olendorf stared grimly at an aide who had just added up the day's casualties. Japan's suicide pilots had sunk one warship, badly damaged eleven others, and killed or injured more than 1,000 officers and sailors. This January sixth had been the deadliest twenty-four hours for the U.S. Navy since Pearl Harbor.

JAN. 8: *Near Malmédy, Belgium*

His eyes ached as Private Herschel Nolan stared out across the snowy fields that glared in the morning sun. His platoon had been trucked here to fill holes in the American line. The German surprise attack across the Ardennes last month had cost Eisenhower's armies almost 50,000 dead and wounded. Most of the dead were riflemen. Nolan had heard his company commander pleading yesterday with battalion headquarters: "Send more 745s." A 745 was an infantry rifleman. Some of the eighteen-year-old riflemen in Nolan's company had been airplane mechanics in Texas a week ago. Planes had flown them across the Atlantic and dropped them here in the front lines.

"Incoming!" a rifleman yelled. Nolan dropped to the ground. The shell exploded in the snow, erupting in red flames and billowing brown smoke. Nolan heard a shriek, turned, and saw blood gushing from a machine gunner a few feet away.

A medic ran to the wounded man. He shook sulfa powder—one of this war's new "miracle" drugs—into the gunner's torn shoulder. Sulfa and other new drugs—like penicillin—stopped infections that had once been killers.

Nolan hacked at the frozen ground with a small shovel, digging a shallow hole to hide from the exploding shells. They were being fired by German mortarmen from a nearby clump of trees.

As he dug, Nolan could see a hand sticking out of a khaki overcoat. The hand belonged to an American soldier, dead for weeks. His was one of more than 150 American bodies found by Nolan's platoon in the past twenty-four hours as they pushed the Germans out of the bulge.

The dead soldiers had been caught by German troops a few hours after the surprise attack through the Ardennes. The soldiers had surrendered. With their hands still raised, they had been cut down by German machine-gun bullets.

From where he crouched in his hole, Nolan could see steam curling upward from the thawing bodies of the massacred GIs. Associated Press war correspondent Hal Boyle joined Nolan in his hole.

"Snow still hides many contorted bodies," Boyle scribbled in his notebook. "Others lie face down or face up, but most of them have their hands upraised where death caught them in an attitude of surprise.

"One soldier clutches his stomach. The back of another soldier's head is blown off. One medic with a bullet hole through his Red Cross armlet lies starkly straight.

"A number of soldiers lie huddled together as if for warmth. The most lifelike is one young red-faced boy who lies on his back with a gloved hand raised childlike to his eyes, as if to ward off a bullet or wipe away a tear."

Boyle and Nolan could see figures walking across the snow toward them, hands upraised. As the figures came closer, Nolan saw they were fifteen German paratroopers. They were being herded by GIs who had found them hiding in the woods.

"The way to do with them is the way they did with us," said Private Bill Babcock to Nolan.

"That's right," Nolan said to Hal Boyle. "They didn't take our men in this field back to any warm chow. If they want to fight that way"—he pointed his rifle toward the slaughtered Americans—"that's OK, but our officers should let us fight the same way."

Herschel Nolan had been a farmer in Oklahoma three years ago. Fewer than one in 100 American fighting men had been soldiers or sailors when World War II began in 1939. They had been drugstore clerks, salesmen, engineers, cops, farmhands, mechanics, teachers, typists.

Few had ever fired a gun, sailed on an ocean ship, or flown in a plane. But they had learned—often in a few months—how to steer ships across oceans, repair complex weapons, pilot fast fighters and huge bombers. Infantrymen like Nolan—they called themselves "dogfaces" or "doggies"—had steeled themselves to plod into curtains of exploding shells and fire back at the enemy. They were firing at German and Japanese professional soldiers who had been fighting wars in Spain or China since 1936.

Most GIs (*GI* meant "Government Issue," a label stamped on their uniforms) dreaded getting up each day to face other men determined to kill them. One of Nolan's officers, Colonel J. C. Farr, told Hal Boyle: "Most GIs look like men who have nothing to look forward to. They can only endure."

"I don't have anything personal against the Germans," one rifleman told Boyle during a

Frozen GIs line up for hot food at a field kitchen during the Battle of the Bulge as Eisenhower struggles to re-form the bulge the Germans punched out in his lines before Christmas. Most soldiers went for as long as a week without hot food during the Bulge. *(Photo courtesy of the National Archives)*

lull in the German shelling. "But I want to kill every German in the world. You know why? To save my own rear end, that's why. But if I make it back home, I tell you this truly: I have a hunting rifle that I know I will never use again. I have seen enough killing to last me a lifetime and then some."

JAN. 9: *Ziegenberg, Germany, Hitler's headquarters*
General Heinz Guderian, Hitler's commander of the eastern front, was pointing to maps. The maps showed the Red Army poised to strike at Hitler's troops defending Germany's eastern border. Guderian pleaded that troops be shifted from the Ardennes in the

west to shore up Germany's eastern wall facing the Red Army.

Guderian knew that he was talking to a dying man. "It was no longer simply his left hand, but the whole left side of his body that trembled," he wrote later. "He walked awkwardly, stooped more than ever, and his gestures were both jerky and slow. He had to have a chair pushed underneath him when he wished to sit down."

Hitler's heart was weakening and his nerves worn raw by drugs he took to sleep. But his doctors feared being shot as "traitors" if they took away the drugs.

Hitler's hypnotic eyes glowed as he listened to Guderian. "The eastern front is like a house of cards," Guderian told Hitler. "If a front is broken through at one point, all the rest will collapse."

Hitler jerked his arms and screamed as he always did when he heard talk of defeat. "No!" he shouted at Guderian. He would send no troops to Guderian. "Your eastern front must . . . make do with what it's got."

Hitler told Guderian that Germany could still win this war. The Americans, British, and Soviets will begin to argue over dividing Europe's riches, he said, "and then we can make peace with one while wiping out the others."

As Hitler talked, said one officer, "there was an indescribable flickering glow in his eyes, creating a fearsome . . . effect."

JAN. 9: *Aboard the cruiser* Boise *in Lingayen Gulf*

General Carlos Romulo watched from the bridge as the biggest armada in history— almost 3,000 warships and landing craft— streamed into the gulf. Some three years earlier, in late December, Carlos Romulo had stood in General Douglas MacArthur's headquarters in Manila. Romulo could still remember what he called "the cold terror" that ran through his body when he heard on Manila radio: "Eighty enemy transports have been sighted in Lingayen Gulf."

Those Japanese invaders had swarmed into Manila and cut off MacArthur's 70,000 Americans and Filipinos on Bataan peninsula. Led by General Tomoyuki Yamashita, the Japanese had besieged the hungry and thirsty men on Bataan and the island fortress of Corregidor. MacArthur escaped to Australia, but his army, commanded by General Jonathan Wainwright, surrendered.

That was 1942. Now it was 1945, and General MacArthur was the attacker, General Yamashita the defender. Now it was MacArthur's warships sailing into Lingayen Gulf. "Now," Romulo said to a soldier, "it is their turn to quake!"

JAN. 10: *On the Lingayen-Manila Road, Luzon*

"It was like we were a carnival—a giant carnival—coming to town."

Sergeant Joe Bennett was writing to a friend

back home. He was describing the landing on Luzon and the march inland toward Manila. Bennett and his platoon of riflemen and machine gunners had waded ashore without hearing a shot being fired. American Hellcat and Mustang fighters droned above them, an umbrella that kept away the now-dreaded kamikazes. Bennett had yet to see a Japanese soldier.

What he did see—by the thousands—were grinning, cheering, flag-waving Filipino men, women, and children. They showered American trucks, tanks, and jeeps with flowers and chanted, "MacArthur! MacArthur!"—a Filipino hero. After three years under the often-brutal Japanese occupiers, the Filipinos welcomed what they called "the Liberators."

Most of MacArthur's 280,000 men had come ashore. Total casualties were five dead and ten wounded. Bennett and his platoon now stood at a dusty crossroads eighty-one miles from Manila. His men were gulping bottles of cold drinks and munching coconuts thrust on them by laughing Filipinos. Bennett told his corporal that somewhere, waiting for them, were Yamashita's 260,000 fighting men. "This fun," Bennett said, "may not last any longer than this road into Manila."

JAN. 12: *Near Czarny Lug on the border of eastern Germany*

The stocky, bearded Marshal Vasili Chuikov, commander of Soviet ground forces, rode in an armored car through the thick morning fog that hung over the rolling ground. Soviet guns had thundered all during the night, blasting freezing German troops dug in behind stone forts near Czarny Lug. The city glued together the thinned-out German line. "If we break through here," Chuikov told his staff, "we will be in Berlin in a month, perhaps even weeks." Berlin was about 200 miles from Czarny Lug.

Chuikov had just left General Georgi Zhukov's headquarters. There he learned that General Eisenhower had sent an urgent request to Stalin: Start an attack in the east that will draw German troops out of the Ardennes in the west. Eisenhower needed more time to replace the riflemen he'd lost during the Battle of the Bulge.

Chuikov's armored car stopped at a Soviet command post. An officer told Chuikov that the guns of German Tiger tanks, massed in Czarny Lug, had blown away Soviet tanks.

"Where are the Katyushi?" Chuikov growled.

The Katyushi were new guns that fired rockets. "After a Katyushi shell explodes," Soviet gunners boasted, "nothing within a city block can be alive—not even a fly."

"A column of Katyushi is coming forward from the east," he was told.

Chuikov climbed into his armored car and rode to meet the column of Katyushi, each gun towed by a truck. He clapped his hands over his ears as thirty-six Katyushi rocketed shells into Czarny Lug.

An hour later he rode into the blasted city. He saw craters where stone houses had stood. Red Army tanks and troops streamed by burning Tigers and blackened corpses.

That night he wrote: "We passed long columns of troops rushing through the gap in the Nazi line. I could see cheerful and laughing faces in the moonlight. . . . They are happy because have broken through . . . we are on our way to Berlin."

JAN. 12: *Washington, the War Department*

Total American casualties in the war had reached 648,380, Secretary of War Henry Stimson told the nation. Almost 140,000 were dead, 370,000 wounded, 63,000 prisoners of war, and almost 75,000 missing in action.

JAN. 18: *Dusseldorf, Germany*

The woman was writing to her soldier son a few hours after American B-17s had bombed the city for the tenth straight day. "We've had hell here. Our town is destroyed to the utmost. Mosel Street and other side streets are a heap of rubble. Everywhere else is too. Aunt Gussie was in Emmerich on Friday and looked all over, but there was no trace of Aunt Mae or Uncle John. All of Emmerich is gone too . . . only a few survivors."

JAN. 20: *New York City*

Mayor Fiorello La Guardia told New Yorkers that meat was scarce. "The Army needs it more than we do," he explained. He was forbidding butchers to sell meat on Mondays, Tuesdays, and Fridays.

Americans had grown accustomed to scarcities. Each man, woman, and child had a ration book with coupons that allowed them to buy items like three or four gallons of gasoline a week, a pound of butter a month, a few ounces of hamburger every other week.

New York City students imitate German soldiers doing a mock goose step during a propaganda display to illustrate how Hitler would enslave the world's youth. *(Photo courtesy of the Library of Congress)*

But lots of mothers were grumbling about the latest item to be rationed. "That's unfair," they said after the War Production Board announced that cotton diapers would have to be kept longer so that two did the work of three.

JAN. 21: *Los Angeles, California*

In 1942 more than 100,000 Japanese-American civilians had been ordered out of their homes along the California coast. The Army, fearing that some might be spies or saboteurs who would blow up war plants, deported them to camps set up in desert areas in California and other western states. Today the War Relocation Board announced that all Japanese-American citizens would be allowed to return to their prewar homes, their loyalty to America no longer doubted.

"There has been a great lessening of anti-Japanese feeling," an official said. "Most Californians have accepted the return of Japanese-Americans from the Relocation Camps as you would expect Americans to do."

JAN. 25: *Near the village of Holtzwihr on the French-German border*

Lieutenant Audie Murphy's Company B riflemen crept across the snow-covered ground in a thick forest. A jagged wind cut at their frozen faces. They had begun their attack on the village this morning with 155 men and six officers. German bullets had whittled down

Company B to two officers and twenty-eight soldiers.

The son of Texas cotton pickers, Audie Murphy had joined Company B as a private in North Africa some two years ago. A skinny five-foot-six-inch bundle of fury, he had fought in North Africa, Sicily, Italy, and now France. Murphy was the only man left of the original 200-man Company B he had joined in 1942. Three of his company commanders had been killed. Audie rose from private to corporal to sergeant. Now he was Lieutenant Murphy. Yesterday another company commander had been killed. Audie Murphy—wounded three times, the winner of the Distinguished Service Medal and a half-dozen other decorations—commanded what was left of Company B.

Crouching in a ditch, Murphy peered through field glasses at a column of German tanks. They were fanning out from the village to try to encircle his small band. Murphy grabbed a field telephone and ordered two tank destroyers to fire at the tanks.

The two tank destroyers raced forward lobbing shells. "Those big German tanks didn't even slow down," a Company B soldier said later.

Heavy German guns were hiding in the village. They boomed shells that crashed into the frozen ground around Murphy's men. Jagged iron and steel fragments screeched through the air. One sliver could tear a man's head off.

A shell blew open the top of one tank destroyer. Men leaped out of its belly, fleeing blue
flames.

Murphy shouted into his field phone, ordering his men to fall back behind a slope a half
mile away. "I couldn't see why all [my men]
had to get killed when one man could do the
job that had to be done," he said later. "And it
was up to me to do it."

Murphy gripped a rifle in one hand and the
phone in the other. He was now watching some
250 Germans advance through the forest behind the tanks. They were wearing their snow-
white camouflage uniforms—GIs called them
"spook suits."

Murphy phoned the positions of the Germans to an artillery spotter. He ordered the
guns to start firing. The spotter asked how
close the Germans were to Murphy.

Snapped Murphy: "Just hold the phone and
I'll let you talk to one of them."

The German troops, Murphy saw, were
steering wide of the burning American tank destroyer. They didn't care to have it explode in
their faces. The tank destroyer now burned behind the advancing Germans.

Murphy jumped out of the ditch and ran to
the tank destroyer. He climbed on top, bent
low, and began to fire the destroyer's heavy,
50-caliber machine gun into the backs of the
Germans. The Germans ran helter-skelter
through the trees, diving into bushes. They

could not see Murphy, shrouded behind flame and smoke.

Perched on his Tiger tank, a German machine gunner saw Murphy atop the destroyer. The tank clanked toward Murphy, its cannon belching fire.

"By now he was completely exposed and silhouetted against the background of bare trees and snow," one Company B soldier, watching from the slope, said later. "There was a fire under him that could blow the destroyer to bits if it reached the gas tank."

The American artillery spotter was listening on the phone for word from Murphy. He could hear bullets whining around Murphy at the other end of the line.

"Are you still alive, Lieutenant?" the artillery sergeant shouted into the phone.

"Momentarily, Sergeant," Murphy said above the roar. "And what are your postwar plans?"

German riflemen now knew a crazy American was blasting bullets at them from the tank destroyer. They moved toward Murphy from four sides.

"If those German infantrymen got within ten yards of the lieutenant," one Company B soldier said, "he killed them . . . wherever he saw them." By now, he guessed, at least thirty-five Germans were dead.

His pants and jackets torn by bullets, Murphy knew he could not stay alive much longer.

He picked up the phone to order American shells to explode right on top of him and the Germans ringed around him. "I figured I could luck out the barrage," he said later. But before he could shout the order, the phone went dead, the line blown away.

Murphy heard a loud droning in the evening's growing darkness. American Mustang fighters had spotted the battle through a break in the low, leaden clouds. The Mustangs zoomed over treetops, firing their cannons. The Germans fled toward the cover of trees.

Murphy crawled off the tank destroyer. His right leg throbbed. A bullet had smashed into the leg. Blood poured down onto his combat boots. He hobbled past dead Germans, his face twisted with pain. Company B soldiers ran toward him, firing their rifles at the retreating Germans.

A sudden roar shook the ground underneath Murphy. He turned to see hunks of the tank destroyer flying through the air. A minute after he had left it, the tank destroyer blew up.

One of the first to shake Murphy's hand was the artillery spotter, Lieutenant Walter Weispfennig. "What you just did," he said, "was the bravest thing I have ever seen a man do in combat." Weispfennig told another officer he would recommend that Murphy be given another medal—this one the nation's highest, the Congressional Medal of Honor.

JAN. 30: *MacArthur's command post, thirty miles from Manila*

General MacArthur was talking to one of his commanders, Lieutenant General Bob Eichelberger. MacArthur told Eichelberger that General Yamashita was pulling his troops out of Manila, retreating into mountains north of Manila.

Navy code breakers had been able to read coded messages sent from Tokyo to Japanese generals and admirals all during the war. Recently the code breakers intercepted a message ordering Yamashita and other generals to execute prisoners of war before the camps were taken by the advancing enemy. Tokyo did not want the world to know of the beheadings, the slow starvation, and the other cruelties that the Japanese inflicted on their prisoners.

Thousands of MacArthur's American and Filipino soldiers, sailors, nurses, and civilians, captured in 1942, were being held in POW camps in Manila.

"Bob," MacArthur said to Eichelberger, "I want you to take two flying columns of First Cavalry troops and dash into Manila and free those prisoners."

Within hours, Eichelberger's armored cars roared toward Manila, filled with 3,000 soldiers. They knew their orders: to free quickly the prisoners in Santo Tomas, Bilbo, and Cabanatuan prisons before the Japanese could kill them.

JAN. 31: *At the Pasig River inside Manila*

For three days Sergeant Joe Bennett had been sitting in the house on the north side of the river. He was watching Japanese tanks scurry back and forth on the river's south bank. Speaking into a field phone, he had given the positions of the tanks so American gunners could blow them up.

"There's that big house with five Japanese on top of it that you could hit," he said on the telephone to an artillery gunner. "And there's a window on the second floor that you guys ought to be able to lay a shot through."

As he spoke, Bennett saw a Japanese tank lumber onto the river's bank, stop, then spin so that its cannon seemed to point directly at Bennett's mouth.

"They spotted us, I think," a soldier said.

The cannon's muzzle flashed red. Bennett ducked. A roaring filled his ears, and the floor shook. A window flew toward him, then the wall of the house.

Bennett and the soldier rose groggily, shaking off plaster and shards of glass. "Let's beat it out of here," Bennett said.

A little later, hiding in a ditch, a captain said to Bennett, "The generals say the Japs are pulling out of Manila. I don't think so."

"I don't think so either," Bennett replied.

Chapter Two

FEB. 2: *Outside the Cabanatuan prison camp near Manila*

The Rangers heard the peeps, whistles, and shrieks of jungle birds as they crawled across the slimy ground. Blood-sucking insects clung to their sweat-streaked, dark-green battle fatigues. Their platoon leader, Lieutenant Bill Connell, glanced at his watch: 7:45 P.M. That was the time for the attack to start.

Silhouetted against the moonlight, Japanese sentries strode back and forth in front of the camp's barbed-wire fences. The sharp crack of a rifle shot echoed in the darkness. Connell saw a sentry topple. "That shot was a signal," he shouted. "Let's go!"

Connell's men swept out of the jungle and ran to the front gate. Their .30-caliber slugs tore apart locks. The gate flew open. The surprised Japanese guards scurried toward small log-walled forts.

The Rangers' red and blue tracer bullets whizzed through the darkness. Splinters flew from the walls of the forts. Rangers ran to the forts and slipped grenades into slits between the logs. The forts blew apart, hunks of log soaring into the night sky.

Connell ran toward a long row of straw huts. Seeing barred windows, he guessed that American prisoners were kept inside.

FEB. 2: *Inside the Cabanatuan prison camp*

Navy Lieutenant Emmet Manson heard the rifle shot and told himself: "That sounded like it was American-made." Prisoners rose weakly from their beds in the dark, steamy hut. Someone shouted hysterically, "The Japs will massacre us before help gets here!"

About forty men were cramped together in this hut. Their faces were thin, pale, sunken cheeked. Rib bones stuck from their bodies, which were covered with sores. Near-starvation meals and diseases like malaria, dysentery, and beriberi had wrung the strength from these once-robust men. Manson had weighed 175 pounds when he was captured on Bataan; now he weighed 115 pounds. For three years he and the other prisoners had been beaten while being made to work from sunup to darkness in blazing heat. They were fed handfuls of rice and slivers of rotting fruit. For daring to look a Japanese soldier in the eyes, they had been clubbed with ax handles and called "white devils." Of more than 5,000 men who had surrendered with Manson in 1942, about 2,700 were dead.

Manson heard more shots echoing outside the hut. He hobbled to a window and saw a log fort in flames. A tall man, dressed in a green uniform, ran by, shouting, "Everybody get to the main gate!"

"We're Americans!" Manson shouted. "We're Americans!"

"I know you are," the man said. "What do you think we are here for?"

Ten minutes later Manson and more than 500 prisoners stood at the gate, ringed by Rangers. The Rangers stared with pity at the gaunt Americans. The tattered sleeves of their dirty uniforms flapped on arms as thin as straws.

Manson could hear the sound of Japanese machine guns coming from the jungle.

"The Japs are coming up the road to the camp," Connell told the prisoners. "We're going to have to force-march you on jungle trails."

"I can't walk," Manson told a Ranger, Sergeant Lyle Fisher. "My ankles are too weak."

"We'll carry you," Fisher said. "None of you looks that heavy."

FEB. 5: *Noyon, France*

P rivate First Class Leroy Kemp was one of more than 25,000 African-American soldiers training here to become infantry riflemen. Most black soldiers in both Europe and the Pacific served as behind-the-front soldiers, laying phone wires, driving trucks, typing, cooking. They served in all-black units in the Army, Navy, and Marines. As civilians, many had

African-American GIs eat at their mess hall. The races lived apart until 1945 when the Army and Navy began to desegregate their combat and noncombat units. In 1944, an all-black infantry division fought with distinction in Italy. *(Photo courtesy of the Library of Congress)*

grown up in racially segregated neighbor-hoods, attended all-black schools, and used blacks-only water fountains and toilets at bus depots and railroad stations. They had joined a wartime military as segregated as peacetime America.

Leroy Kemp had been a truck driver in an all-black service unit. Two weeks ago he had volunteered to fight as a rifleman. Eisenhower needed riflemen. Thousands of riflemen had been lost in the Battle of the Bulge. Kemp and thousands of other black volunteers would soon join all-white infantry companies. An all-black infantry division—some 20,000 men—was fighting the Germans in Italy, as were all-black fighter-pilot squadrons. But now, for the first time in World War II, African-Americans would be officially fighting side by side with white soldiers.

"We're all in this together now," Private Kemp was telling a writer for the Army newspaper, *Stars and Stripes*. "There are white and Negro Americans in the same companies now, and that's how it should be. Most of us Negro soldiers have been in back-of-the-lines service units. We've been giving a lot of sweat. Now, I think, we'll mix some blood with it."

FEB. 8: *Old Bilibid Prison, Manila*

"**A**ttention!" shouted an officer. Men jumped to their feet and stood erect as General MacArthur strode into the smelly, dimly lit room. It had been a jail for American prisoners until three days ago, when Rangers had smashed into the prison and killed the Japanese guards. MacArthur had come here to greet some of the men he had left behind on Bataan and Corregidor in 1942.

MacArthur asked the haggard former prisoners to sit down. He stared at their wasted bodies. "The men who greeted me were scarcely more than skeletons," he said later.

"You're back!" one soldier called out in a

croaking voice. "You made it!" someone else shouted.

MacArthur's eyes were moist. "I'm a little late," he said, "but we finally came."

FEB. 11: *Yalta, a port in the Crimea region of the USSR*

B urning logs crackled in the fireplace. Uniformed butlers hurried across the marble floors of the palace, carrying plates of caviar. They set the plates in front of Josef Stalin's two guests. One was the ruddy-faced Winston Churchill. The other was a pale Franklin D. Roosevelt, seated in a stiff-backed chair, a blanket covering his legs. The stumpy, mustached Stalin roared with laughter as he shouted the few English words he knew: "So what! You said it! The toilet is over there!"

Churchill did not join in the laughter. He stared gloomily at Roosevelt. Churchill's doctor, Lord Moran, had told Churchill that the sixty-three-year-old Roosevelt was a dying man. "He has all the symptoms of hardening of the brain arteries," Moran told Churchill. "A stroke could kill him instantly."

"He looks so pale and drawn you feel you can see through him," Churchill told a friend.

Roosevelt had come to this Yalta Conference of the Big Three to talk Stalin into declaring war on Japan after Germany was defeated. Stalin quickly agreed. But he told Roosevelt and Churchill that most of eastern Europe—Poland,

The big three—Churchill, Roosevelt, Stalin—meet at Yalta more to discuss the political carving up of Europe than to reach any military decisions. Stalin did agree to join the war against Japan. *(Photo courtesy of the National Archives)*

Bulgaria, Czechoslovakia, Rumania, Estonia, Latvia, and Lithuania—had been won with the blood of Soviet soldiers. His soldiers, he said, would stay in those countries after the war.

An angry Churchill told Roosevelt they must stop the spread of what Churchill called "Stalin's bloody communism." Churchill winced as he saw Roosevelt nod off during their talks. He growled to aides that Roosevelt would "do anything to get Stalin into the war against the Japanese."

Roosevelt's wife, Eleanor, had told him that the people of the United States would not want to see the people of eastern Europe living under Stalin's iron hand.

Roosevelt shrugged. He reminded his wife that eastern Europe was overrun by the Red Army. "How many people in the United States," he asked her, "do you think would be willing to go to war to free Estonia, Latvia, and Lithuania?"

FEB. 15: *Chequers, the country home of Prime Minister Churchill*

Air Marshal Arthur Harris was dining with Churchill, who had just come back from Yalta. For weeks Churchill had angrily demanded that Harris order the Royal Air Force to bomb the German city of Dresden, even though there were no war factories inside the city. Dresden had been famous since the Middle Ages for its delicate glass dolls, ornate statues, and postcard-pretty houses.

Harris had asked Churchill why Dresden should be bombed. Each German city, Churchill growled, had to feel the wrath of the Allies.

During the past twenty-four hours Harris had sent 2,000 bombers over Dresden. They had dropped 650,000 firebombs. Harris estimated that more than 130,000 Germans had died. Most, he said, suffocated to death as mile-high flames sucked all the oxygen out of Dresden.

Churchill listened but said nothing, even as Harris told him that the bombing had killed more people than any one attack in history.

John Colville, Churchill's secretary, entered the room and asked, "What is the news of Dresden?"

"There is no longer any such place as Dresden," Harris said.

FEB. 17: *Atop Mount Suribachi on Iwo Jima, the headquarters of General Tadamichi Kuribayashi*

"The Americans will take this island," the squat, potbellied Kuribayashi was telling his officers. "This island is their gateway to Japan."

Iwo Jima, a five-mile-by-three-mile dot in the Pacific, sat only 750 miles from Tokyo. The Americans, Kuribayashi knew, would use Iwo Jima as a base for fighter planes. Until now, the American fighters could not protect their B-29s as they dropped bombs on Japan; the fighters did not have the range to fly from Guam to Japan. But if they could take off from Iwo Jima, they could meet the B-29s, guard them over Japan, then fly back to this island.

The Americans must pay heavily for Iwo Jima, Kuribayashi said. His 22,000 troops had dug concrete-lined tunnels coiled inside 556-foot-high Suribachi. Huge naval guns poked out of the mouths of those tunnels. Their muzzles stared down on the flat, mushy-soft beaches where, Kuribayashi said, at least 200,000 Americans would soon land.

His guns, Kuribayashi told his officers, could not hold off the Americans forever. "But American blood," he said, "must run down from this peak to the beaches in such torrents that the Americans must hesitate before they will dare to invade Japan."

He had just written a battle order to his troops. "The Americans," he told his soldiers, "will cut off the left arm of each Japanese they capture and make it into a letter opener to be sent to their president. And Japanese heads will be cut off to make into American ashtrays."

His order ended: "We would all like to die quickly and easily, but that would not inflict heavy casualties on the invaders who will next try to attack our homeland."

An hour later twenty-two-year-old Private Shigeru Yoshida was reading the order. Yoshida stood behind a row of huge guns taken from damaged Japanese warships. He snapped to attention as an officer began to address Yoshida and the other gunners.

"The cross fire of our guns will be so murderous," the officer said, "that no American will be able to stand up on that beach without having his head taken off."

Yoshida then took this vow with the rest of his battery: "Each man will kill ten of the enemy before dying."

FEB. 19: *On the beach at Iwo Jima*

S ergeant Charley Anderson, Jr., was clawing a hole in the ashy beach as exploding mortar shells threw up black geysers around him. As fast as he and other marines dug, the ash crumbled and their holes collapsed. They lay with their faces in the foul-smelling ash as bullets and shells streamed down from Suribachi.

Charley Anderson and his rifle platoon were among the first ashore. More than 30,000 marines bobbed in boats behind them. Black ash cinders pelted bleeding faces and rained down on torn bodies. Litter bearers crawled—no one dared to stand—among the screaming wounded. They tugged dying men toward boats they had left minutes ago.

Anderson and the other surviving marines stared at towering cliffs rising above the beaches. An officer told them that the marines had to charge up the cliffs. "We're all dead men," he shouted, "if we stay here."

Anderson stumbled on the slippery ash as he ran toward the cliffs. He was gasping in the steamy, stinking air. The volcanic ash gave off fumes that smelled like rotten eggs. He tried to scramble up a ten-foot-high hill of sand. "It was like trying to climb a waterfall," one of Anderson's friends said later. Anderson slipped backward, his feet kicking against bullet-torn bodies of marines who had died seconds ago.

The saucer-shaped land mine, buried in the sand, exploded as Anderson nudged it with his boot. Hunks of jagged iron tore his legs. Litter bearers carried him, moaning and half-conscious, to a boat. Filled with the wounded, dead, and dying, the landing boat crawled toward a hospital ship.

Other marines were coming ashore and sinking up to their knees in the ash. One marine later wrote of men "leaving behind footprints of an elephant, the sand tugging legs like quicksand. . . . Tanks chugged as though caught in tarpaper . . . and all you smelled was the sulphurous odor of rotting eggs."

FEB. 19: *Manila*

Sergeant Bob Steele scooted across the roof of the factory building, clutching a can of gasoline. He set down the can. He blasted holes in the roof with a burst of bullets from his M-3 submachine gun. He poured gasoline down the holes, hearing frightened shouts from the floor below him. Japanese snipers were trying to find where the shots were coming from.

Steele flipped grenades down the holes. He ran to the roof of another building as the exploding grenades shook the factory. Orange and bluish flames spurted through the holes in the roof.

"We learned quickly in Manila," he said later to a war correspondent, "that you battle for a building by going from the top down, not from the bottom up. When you go in at the bottom, they shoot at you from the second floor. When you clear out the second floor, they shoot at you from the third floor."

General Yamashita had ordered his troops to retreat from Manila, a city so beautiful it was called the Pearl of the Orient. But a Japanese rear admiral, Sanji Iwabuchi, had refused to follow Yamashita's troops into the mountains. Iwabuchi ordered his 30,000 sailors and marines to defend the city building by building.

Caught in the cross fire were Filipino men, women, and children. Drunken Japanese sailors smashed into houses, raping women and bayoneting babies. The Japanese stormed into hospitals, slaughtering patients whose bodies were turned into barricades.

"Never has the hatred for the Japanese soldier been as deep among GIs as here in Manila," a soldier-writer declared in the Army's *Yank* magazine. "What they did to the people of Manila—more than 100,000 Filipino men and women and children dead—will never be forgotten by the men who retook the Pearl of the Orient."

FEB. 19: *Aboard a ship off Iwo Jima*

N avy Captain Charles Anderson, Sr., watched as the wounded marines were lifted off the landing craft and carried onto the deck of his ship. He recognized his son, Sergeant Charley Anderson, Jr. One look told the father that his son was badly wounded, both legs shattered by a mine.

Sergeant Anderson saw his father standing over him. "I'm feeling pretty good," Sergeant Anderson said. Then he gazed at his father and said, "I wonder how Mother will take all this." Seconds later he was dead.

FEB. 22: *Iwo Jima*

Marine medic Jack Williams crawled across the black, stinking slope toward the shell crater. Even from 100 yards away, amid ground-shaking explosions, he could hear the shrieks of someone wounded inside the crater.

A bullet kicked up sand in front of him, then to his side. Williams jumped up and ran, knowing a sniper—one he couldn't see—had him in his sights. He zigzagged toward the crater. Three bullets slammed into his ribs, but he staggered on and tumbled into the crater.

The wounded marine had stopped shrieking. Williams saw he was still alive. Face twisted in pain, Williams wrapped bandages and put sulfa drugs on the marine's riddled body. Then he bandaged his own torn side, using wads of cotton to stop the gushing blood.

"I'll be back with a stretcher bearer," Williams told the wounded man. He slid out of the crater and wormed toward a first-aid station. A wounded man's moaning stopped him. He patched up that man's wounds.

"I'll be back for you with a stretcher," he told the wounded man. The wounded man saw blood spilling down onto Williams's boots.

A marine dashes across barren terrain—a suicide zone on Iwo Jima—as the marines scratch and claw their way up the ashy slope toward the island's peak. *(Photo courtesy of the National Archives)*

Moments later another sniper's bullet caught Williams in the back and killed him instantly.

By now—only three days after landing on Iwo Jima—more than 3,000 marines were dead, at least 4,000 wounded. And only half of this fifteen-square-mile island had been cleared of its defenders. Countless Japanese still hid in a thousand caves and tunnels. Their rifles, machine guns, and battleship guns looked straight down at marines slipping and sliding as they crawled foot by foot up Suribachi's slopes.

FEB. 22: *Washington, D.C., War Production Board headquarters*

WPB officials smiled as they left the room. For the first time, there was now enough penicillin, they had just learned, to supply all the needs of the armed forces. The "wonder drug" had proved it could save the lives of wounded fighting men. Now it would be available to save the lives of America's sick civilians. One New York doctor told the WPB that penicillin "can save more lives at home in the next twelve months than it has saved on all the fighting fronts around the globe."

FEB. 23: *Near the Manila Hotel, Manila*

General MacArthur had insisted on joining a platoon of infantrymen, carrying machine guns, as they attacked the hotel. It was held by Japanese sailors who had refused to surrender. Before the war MacArthur had lived in this hotel's penthouse with his wife, Jean, and their son, Arthur.

MacArthur crouched low as he followed a lieutenant, carrying a submachine gun, into the hotel's lobby. Machine-gun bullets spattered against a wall behind him. He followed three soldiers as they climbed the stairs, hearing the roar of guns from the floors above them.

"The higher the stairs," an aide wrote, "the warmer the bodies were, and I was afraid one of them might be just wounded, or shamming."

"Every landing was a fight," MacArthur later said. "[The penthouse] had evidently been the command post. We left its colonel dead."

Inside the smoking, shattered penthouse,

the lieutenant put down his submachine gun and said to his commanding general, "Nice going, Chief."

"But there was nothing nice about it to me," MacArthur later said. "I was tasting . . . the bitterness of a devastated and beloved home."

MacArthur walked through a Manila "dripping with the blood of innocents," a MacArthur aide said later. His foe, General Yamashita, was preparing to fight for months in Luzon's craggy mountains, but the battle for the Philippines had ended when burning, smashed Manila was safe in American hands. MacArthur's engineers were rebuilding Manila's docks and the island of Luzon's air bases. They would be the springboards for MacArthur's leap northward 600 miles to Japan.

FEB. 23: *Mount Suribachi, Iwo Jima*

A marine raised his helmeted head warily as he stared upward at the top of Suribachi. For hours he and five other marines had lobbed mortar shells and sprayed machine-gun bullets at Japanese gunners holding Suribachi's crest. "Take Suribachi," one marine said, "and we crawl out of this island's sand and up into the sky."

The six marines moved stealthily up steep slopes to the crest. They could hear the faraway thump, crackle, and roar of battles on the slopes below them. But up here they heard only the whine of the wind.

They reached the crest and saw torn Japanese bodies, strewn around wrecked guns. One of the marines pulled from a pocket a small American flag. He tied it to a pipe stuck into the ground. A marine sergeant, Louis Lowery, took a snapshot of the marines gathered around the flag.

"Look out!" someone yelled.

The marines whirled to see two Japanese running toward them. One was waving a saber. A marine killed him with a rifle shot. The second Japanese hurled a grenade at Lowery, who dived into a crater. As the grenade exploded

Raising their flag high above the Pacific they have conquered, five U.S. Marines join in celebration as the flag is mounted over Iwo Jima's Mount Suribachi. The flag was hoisted, but the battle was not yet won, and four of these five men would later be killed or wounded. *(Photo courtesy of the National Archives)*

above Lowery, bullets ripped into the body of the grenade thrower, killing him.

An hour later Associated Press photographer Jack Rosenthal climbed to the top of Suribachi, guarded by a patrol of riflemen. They brought with them a huge American flag that was tied to a long pole. Six marines pushed at the pole, swinging it upward so that the Stars and Stripes swirled in the winds above Iwo Jima. Rosenthal snapped a picture.

FEB. 26: *Washington, D.C.*

Mrs. Charles Anderson heard the doorbell ring. She opened the door and saw the grim face of a Navy chaplain. She asked quickly, "Is it my husband or my son?"

"Your son," the chaplain said. Marine Sergeant Charles Anderson had been killed in action.

"A force stronger than ours has taken charge," she said calmly. That afternoon she drove to her volunteer's job caring for the wounded at Bethesda Naval Hospital.

FEB. 26: *San Francisco, California*

Riding in trolley cars on their way to work, *San Francisco Chronicle* readers saw a front-page photograph by Jack Rosenthal of the Associated Press. It showed marines hoisting the flag high above Iwo Jima. The *Chronicle*'s caption writer predicted that the photo would become "the most famous of all the photos showing our men in the Pacific."

Chapter Three

Saipan, headquarters of the Fifth Air Force Bombing Command

"No guns!" the captain exclaimed. "General, the B-29 crews won't like that!"

He was speaking to Major General Curtis LeMay, the beefy, cigar-puffing commander of the B-29s now taking off each day from here and Guam to bomb Japan. America's top war planner, General George C. Marshall, had sent LeMay to the Far East with one mission: to bomb Japan into surrender so that American troops would not have to invade Japan. Marshall feared that an invasion of Japan would cost at least one million American casualties.

"Tokyo is a city of wooden buildings," LeMay told his B-29 pilots and bombardiers. "But to set Tokyo afire, we have to drop the firebombs closer to the targets."

That meant rooftop bombing by the B-29s—a tactic that LeMay hoped would surprise the Japanese. Their antiaircraft guns were aimed to fire at planes above 20,000 feet. "If you come in low," he told the B-29 crews, "they can't hit you because you're moving too fast."

To make the B-29s faster, LeMay ordered the planes stripped of all weapons. "Anyway you won't need the guns," he told worried pilots, "you'll be guarded against fighter attacks by fighters coming from Iwo Jima."

The first low-level bombing was set for early March. The target would be twelve square miles of workers' houses.

"Ninety percent of the target area is populated by civilians," one bombardier told LcMay.

"No matter how you slice it," LeMay said, "you're going to kill an awful lot of civilians. But if you don't destroy Japanese industry, we're going to have to invade Japan. Do you want to kill Japanese, or would you rather have a million Americans killed invading Japan?"

MARCH 1: *Dresden, Germany*

Private Kurt Vonnegut, an American rifle-man, had been captured by the Germans during the Battle of the Bulge. He and other American prisoners were being ordered by their guards to drag corpses from under Dresden's burned-out buildings after the British bombing three weeks ago. The nineteen-year-old Kurt wanted to be a writer. He had been scribbling notes about the burning of a city he had come to admire and the deaths by suffocation of at least 100,000. "Dresden," he would later say, "[was] a city full of statues and zoos, like Paris. We never expected to get hit. There were very few air-raid shelters in town. . . .

"Every day we walked into the city and dug to get corpses out, as a sanitary measure. When we went into a typical shelter, an ordinary basement usually, [it looked] like a streetcar full of people who'd simultaneously had heart failure. Just people sitting in their chairs, all dead. We brought the dead out. They were loaded onto wagons and taken to parks. . . . The Germans got funeral pyres going, burning the bodies to keep them from stinking and spreading disease."

MARCH 1: *Washington, Capitol Hill*

The members of the House and Senate stood to applaud President Roosevelt as he entered the chamber.

He had come with a "personal report," he said, on his trip to Yalta for the Big Three meeting. As he talked, the senators and congressmen stared intently at his drawn, pale face.

Next month, he said, delegates from around the world would meet in San Francisco to form a peacekeeping United Nations organization. America and the new UN, he said, are "responsible for keeping the peace. We must cooperate with other nations or bear the responsibility for another world conflict."

Applause filled the chamber as he finished.

But in a hallway, a congressman whispered that "the President does not look well at all."

MARCH 2: *On a hill seven miles from Bologna, Italy*

Sergeant Bill Mauldin, a correspondent for *Stars and Stripes,* watched as the wounded rifleman was carried into the medical-aid station. Rain sliced against the windows of the wooden shack. Mauldin could hear the rattle of machine guns from the valley below the shack.

This, he told himself, is "the forgotten front." American, Canadian, and British troops had pushed the Germans north to Germany's border with Italy. But people back home were watching for news from Germany that Berlin had fallen.

As Mauldin stood nearby, a doctor cut off the wounded soldier's bloody shirt and pants. "His face was a pulp," Mauldin later wrote, "and one arm and a leg were shattered and riddled."

"God, I'm hurtin'," the wounded man screamed. "Give me a shot."

"We gave you a shot," a medic said. "Just a minute, and you'll feel better."

"What got you, Jack?" the doctor asked. He had read the soldier's name on the dogtags around his neck.

"It was a grenade," Jack said, reaching a hand to feel his shattered face. "Where's the chaplain? Doc, why do you let me hurt like this?"

"You won't need a chaplain, you'll be OK." The doctor asked for his age. "Twenty," the soldier gasped. He was a staff sergeant from Texas.

"I looked at the holes which had riddled his right arm and practically severed his little finger," Mauldin wrote. "And I looked at the swollen bloody gashes on his leg. I looked at his horribly wounded face and head, and I thought of how twenty minutes ago he was sitting quietly in his hole and wondering how soon he could get home."

An hour later Jack was being lifted into an ambulance. "Jack's face was fixed and it didn't look so bad with a neat bandage," Mauldin wrote. "He was full of morphine and probably dreaming of home."

MARCH 2: *Washington, the Census Bureau*

Despite World War II's death toll, an official disclosed, America's population had grown during the war years. "For every man killed in battle since Pearl Harbor," he said, "twelve babies have been born."

MARCH 7: *Remagen, Germany*

"Do you think your company can get across that bridge?" the American major asked the rangy lieutenant.

Lieutenant Karl Timmerman stared through the misty rain at the railroad bridge that crossed the choppy Rhine River. Timmerman was crouched on the west side of the river. He could see the barrels of German guns aiming at him from the east bank's steep slope.

For two centuries the swift-flowing currents of the Rhine had been a graveyard for armies trying to cross into Germany. Hitler had ordered that all Rhine bridges be blown up. But an American patrol had seen that this bridge still stood. If the Americans could cross, Eisenhower's armies could pour across the Rhine — Hitler's last defense — and streak for Berlin.

The major was asking Timmerman and his men to cross the bridge before the Germans could blow it up. Lieutenant Timmerman's 200 riflemen and machine gunners were the only troops here.

"Well," Timmerman said slowly and reluctantly, "we can try, sir."

MARCH 7: *On the east side of the bridge at Remagen*

"Blow up the bridge!" German Captain Will Bratge shouted at the explosives engineer.

The engineer looked at his watch. The time was a little past 3:00 P.M. The engineer had strict orders not to blow up the bridge before 4:00 P.M. Hitler had ordered the execution of anyone who blew up a Rhine bridge too soon.

The engineer told Bratge he had to wait until four.

Bratge could see helmeted GIs moving in single file toward the bridge. "If you don't give the order to blow the bridge," shouted Bratge, "I'll give it!"

A minute later, Bratge heard dull roars echoing from under the steel girders of the bridge. Strings of dynamite sticks, strapped to the belly of the bridge, began to explode.

MARCH 7: *On the west side of the bridge at Remagen*

L ieutenant Timmerman heard the roaring, then saw the bridge heave upward.

"We can't cross the bridge," he shouted to his riflemen. "It's just been blown."

"Now we get five days' rest," a sergeant said happily to himself.

Timmerman ran to a slope to get a better view of the collapsed bridge. He heard a soldier murmur in an awed voice: "She's still standing."

The Germans, Timmerman guessed, had skimped on the dynamite needed to blow up a railroad bridge.

"All right, we cross the bridge," Timmerman shouted to his men. "Let's go."

Machine-gun slugs sang above their helmets as the riflemen stepped onto the bridge. Timmerman knew the weakened bridge could snap at any moment, dropping them 100 feet into the deep, fast-flowing river.

"I don't want to go," one soldier was muttering as he followed Timmerman, "but I will."

MARCH 7: *Paris, Supreme Headquarters American Expeditionary Force (SHAEF)*

Eisenhower was shouting into the telephone to one of his army commanders, General Omar Bradley. Ike had just been told that an infantry company had crossed the Rhine at Remagen, seizing the only bridge still hanging over the river.

"Go ahead and shove over at least five divisions instantly," Ike told Bradley. "Make certain we hold that bridge."

Eisenhower hung up. When he had heard that a Rhine bridge had been taken, he said, "I could hardly believe my ears."

Now Bradley could cross the Rhine, then strike north to link up with "Blood and Guts" Patton's Third Army. Patton and Bradley, Eisenhower hoped, could seal off more than 250,000 Germans guarding the Rhine along Hitler's vaunted West Wall, Germany's last line before Berlin. "This," Ike told an aide, "is one of the happiest moments of the war."

MARCH 9: *Berlin, Hitler's bunker under the garden of the Reich Chancellory*

Field Marshal Albert Kesselring was called "Smiling Al" by his aides because an angry frown nearly always hung from his monocled face. Now, however, his face showed surprise as he was led down the steep steps of this concrete-walled underground bunker.

He had been stunned by the size of the

three-level bunker. It was big enough to hold more than 200 of Hitler's staff—secretaries, cooks, his generals, Propaganda Minister Joseph Goebbels and his wife and six children, plus Hitler and his woman friend, Eva Braun.

Kesselring had slowed the push of the Allied armies in Italy toward Germany. Now, a twitching Hitler told him, he would take command of Hitler's armies along the West Wall to stop Eisenhower's stab into Germany.

"Only a commander like you, who has had experience fighting the Western powers," Hitler told a grim-faced Kesselring, "can perhaps still restore the situation."

Kesselring feared it was too late to plug the hole in the West Wall at Remagen. But he shouted, "Heil Hitler!" He flung up his right arm in the Nazi salute to a tottering Führer, then left the bunker for the Rhine.

Hitler slumped in a chair. He dictated an order: All officers who had failed to blow up the Remagen bridge were to be shot by firing squads.

MARCH 9: *West Point, New York*

Mary Timmerman, a waitress at the Goldenrod Café, was summoned to the phone. Calling was a reporter. He told Mary that her son, Karl, had commanded the GIs who had captured the bridge at Remagen.

"Is he hurt?" she asked.

"No, he is not hurt," the reporter said. "But

listen to this, Mrs. Timmerman. Your son was the first officer of an invading army to cross the Rhine since Napoleon."

"Napoleon I don't care about," Mary Timmerman said. "How is my Karl?"

MARCH 10: *5,000 feet over Tokyo*

The first wave of General LeMay's silver-winged B-29s sped over the darkened city. It was a little after midnight. The pilots could see flames forming a huge white and red cross. That burning cross had been set ablaze by the firebombs of B-29s crisscrossing the city an hour earlier. The cross marked the targets— Tokyo's wooden workers' houses—for LeMay's firebombs.

"Bombs away . . . bombs away . . . bombs away." That shout crackled over earphones as bombardiers dropped thousands of sticks of firebombs. The bombardiers could see a huge bowl of white-hot flame where buildings once stood. Fiery-hot bubbles of air rose to toss the B-29s like sticks.

Then came a second wave of the B-29s, then third and fourth waves. As LeMay had predicted, the B-29s were zooming too fast and too low to be caught between the crosshairs of antiaircraft gunners.

MARCH 10: *Arakawam, a suburb of Tokyo*

The boy's name was Wakabayashi. It was a little after 2:00 A.M., and the ear-blasting roar of the B-29s had faded to the south as he crawled out of his basement shelter.

As he stepped into the street, a fireball struck his arm, searing his hand. Blisters popped up on the hand. He heard calls for help and raced to a burning building, gripping a *hi-tataki*. It was a bamboo pole tipped with water-soaked cotton. He jabbed at the flames with the pole, but the heat singed his face. He ran toward a nearby river.

He stopped at the river's bank. He saw people packed shoulder to shoulder in the water, standing as upright as row after row of celery stalks. All were dead, held up by the stiffening bodies of the thousands who had fled to the river to escape the heat. Most had suffocated to death, the 1,800-degree flames sucking oxygen out of the air.

Wakabayashi came to a stream. Bodies floated on top of the bubbling water. The fires had heated the stream into a cauldron in which hundreds of men, women, and children were boiled to death.

MARCH 12: *Tokyo, the Imperial Palace*

The eyes behind the thick glasses were filled with sadness. Emperor Hirohito, sitting on his throne, listened to a report on the firebombing two nights ago. The bombs had killed at least 100,000 and badly burned at least another 40,000. More than one million were homeless, their houses incinerated into ashes.

"Whole neighborhoods have just vanished," an official told the Emperor. Never before in the history of humankind, he said, had so many people been killed in so short a time—fewer than three hours.

MARCH 12: *Iwo Jima*

The rangy marine, Lieutenant Jack Lummus, had snared passes for Baylor's football team. He hoped to play with the pro football New York Giants after the war. His E Company had fought its way yard by yard to this rocky shore. "A half-a-mile gain a day was enormous," one marine said. Here the last of Kuribayashi's defenders were hiding in caves.

Two and a half weeks after the invasion of Iwo Jima had begun, 50,000 marines had landed. Almost 5,000 were dead and another 25,000 wounded. In only two days of fighting, seven of every ten men in one battalion had been killed or wounded.

Lummus's riflemen and machine gunners had formed a ring around a hill that ran down to the sea. Japanese riflemen hurled grenades as the marines crawled around boulders.

Lummus, crouching behind a boulder, saw the muzzle of a Japanese machine gun spit fire from a cave. He jumped up and slid along the rocks toward the mouth of the cave, gripping an M-3 submachine gun.

A grenade exploded at his feet. Shards of metal slashed Lummus's legs. He staggered, trying to keep on moving toward the cave. Another grenade blew up behind him, tearing off part of his left shoulder. Lummus was wobbling as he stood in front of the cave, tossing grenades with his good right arm. Smoke billowed from the cave. Through the smoke Lummus saw six Japanese bodies.

He waved to riflemen to follow him to a higher cave. Within the next hour the marines had blown Japanese gunners out of four caves. At the top of the hill, gasping, the marines looked down at the churning sea, their battle for Iwo Jima finally ended.

On a slope below them, both legs blown away by a cannon shell, Jack Lummus lay dying.

MARCH 18: *Guam, General LeMay's Twentieth Air Force headquarters*

Chewing on a cigar that was unlit, the chunky LeMay was dictating a message to his boss in Washington, General Henry ("Hap") Arnold. His gamble had paid off, he told Arnold, the Air Corps chief. In the past ten days, he said, his B-29s' firebombs had charred cities like Nagoya, Osaka, and Kobe. The firebombs, he estimated, had killed at least 150,000.

Let me go on firebombing Japan, LeMay told Hap Arnold, and Japan will beg to surrender. There would be no need for an invasion.

MARCH 19: *Tokyo*

The kamikaze pilots were being briefed on their target. Their faces showed their surprise. They had just been told that their target was hundreds of American ships steaming toward the island of Okinawa.

Okinawa! That island sat only 360 miles from Japan's shores. It was the home of 750,000 Japanese farmers. The American fleet, the pilots were told, carried 200,000 marines and soldiers who would slaughter the Japanese farmers and their families.

Dive on the warships, blow yourself up on the decks of transports, an officer told the pilots. "It is absolutely out of the question for you to return alive," he shouted. "Your mission involves certain death. Choose a death that kills the most Americans and sinks the most ships. The enemy now stands at our front gate. It is the gravest moment of our country's history."

MARCH 23: *Washington, D.C., the White House*

President Roosevelt sat in his wheelchair, staring moodily out of the window into the Rose Garden. He had been chatting with Secretary of Labor Frances Perkins, an old friend and the first woman ever to be a member of a president's cabinet.

Perkins had never seen Roosevelt looking so worn out. But there was a note of excitement in his voice as he told her that he would go to

San Francisco next month to speak to the first meeting of the United Nations organization.

He worried, he said, about Stalin's delegates to the UN. They wanted, he said, the right to veto any idea they didn't like. And they said *nyet* (the Russian word for "no") to free elections in Poland and other eastern European countries.

"Averell is right," Roosevelt said, banging his fist on the arms of his wheelchair. Averell Harriman, Roosevelt's envoy to Moscow, had warned him that Stalin was building a wall of Communist-ruled states across eastern Europe. "We can't do business with Stalin," Roosevelt said angrily. "He has broken every one of the promises he made at Yalta."

His face brightened. He told Perkins he would leave within the next few days to go to his favorite resort, Warm Springs, Georgia. There he liked to bathe his disease-withered limbs in the warming spring waters. He would finish writing his UN speech at Warm Springs, he told Perkins.

MARCH 26: *Iwo Jima*

Japanese soldier Toshihiko Ohno was hiding in the cave with three other soldiers. He watched the American marine scaling the rocks, clutching a flamethrower. Ohno winced when he saw the flamethrower. Those "guns from hell," as the Japanese called them, spurted tongues of flame to burn alive Japanese burrowed inside caves. This marine, he saw, had pulled out a grenade. The marine hurled the grenade. Ohno and his fellow machine gunners dived onto the floor of a tunnel inside the cave.

The grenade blew up a few feet from Ohno, showering white phosphorus powder onto his back. Ohno leaped up and began brushing off the powder. This stuff, he knew, burst into flames, ignited by body heat, within seconds.

"Hurriedly we took off our clothes and rubbed them in the dirt," he said later. "But when we managed to scrape the phosphorus off our clothes, we found it starting to run under our nails. If we got it off the right hand, the left hand would start to burn. For four or five hours we battled the phosphorus and we completely forgot about the Americans."

The American marines camped for the night about 300 yards away. Ohno could smell the candylike scent of the toothpaste they liked.

"We could hear them talking. It was always dangerous for us to let cooking smoke come from a cave. But since the grenade still let out smoke, I took the opportunity to cook our food properly and we enjoyed a beautifully cooked dinner that day. We talked about home and even managed to have some laughs."

The battle for Iwo Jima had officially ended on March 16. After twenty-seven days of fighting on this fifteen-square-mile cone of ash, 21,000 Japanese and almost 7,000 Americans were dead. The death list was the longest for any battle area this small in the history of human warfare. Total marine and navy casualties—dead, wounded, blown away, and forever missing in action—added up to 27,000. Of the six men who had raised the Stars and Stripes over Mount Suribachi, two had been wounded and three were dead.

The time was now near midnight, the marine camp quiet. Ohno and the three gunners decided to die for Japan—but to take some Americans with them. They crept toward the marine tents, gripping bayonets. A guard saw Ohno in the moonlight. A .30-caliber bullet whizzed by Ohno's ear.

Ohno leaped through the door of a tent and dived under a cot. He could hear a marine snoring above him. Ohno raised the bayonet over the sleeping marine's chest. Pain shot through his back "as though I had been hit by a flying telegraph pole. I was tumbling over the rocky ground, the bayonet gone."

A marine had tackled him. Ohno and two of his gunners—the third was killed—were among the 1,000 Japanese who were captured or who surrendered on Iwo Jima. The total was more than all of the Japanese captured so far in the war.

Ohno had expected to be tortured. Instead he was fed and treated for his burns. He had begun to wonder, he said, if his Iwo Jima comrades had done the sensible thing when they chose to die rather than surrender.

Chapter Four

APRIL 1: *Moscow, the Kremlin*

A British-made pipe clenched between his teeth, the stocky Josef Stalin stood at the head of a long table. Seated on both sides of the table, facing him, were his top generals, including his favorite commander, Georgi Zhukov.

Stalin told them that he had received a message from Eisenhower that the Allied armies were now aiming at southern Germany. Eisenhower said he believed Hitler would dig in there for a last-ditch fight.

One of Stalin's generals roared laughter. He did not believe Ike, he said. "Eisenhower's main aim," he said, "is to take Berlin."

Stalin nodded. The Americans wanted what Stalin wanted, to be the first to enter Berlin. Whoever owned Berlin would be the boss when the Allies carved up Germany and the rest of eastern Europe after the war.

The barrel-chested Zhukov stood up. He announced proudly that his armies were the shortest distance from Berlin, about fifty miles.

"We will take Berlin," he promised Stalin. "We will get there before the Americans."

APRIL 2: *A town on the Rhine*

Sergeant Francis Mitchell led his squad of riflemen through the rubble that had once been an alley built in the fifteenth century. The eyes of the dogfaces, as they called themselves, scanned shattered windows looking for snipers. Mitchell's riflemen were the scouts for an American army advancing along the Rhine to meet troops who had crossed the river at Remagen. Sandwiched between the Americans were more than 250,000 defenders of Hitler's West Wall.

Mitchell heard a baby crying. German women, children, and old men were climbing up from cellars. Seeing the Americans, they begged for food. For a week, one man told Mitchell, they had hidden underground as shells whizzed over the town.

Eisenhower had ordered his troops not to become friendly with German civilians. "They are the enemy," his order stated.

Most frontline doggies, like Mitchell, were ignoring the order. "The civilians," Mitchell told a correspondent, "are mostly children and old people—just sort of helpless and glad they were not being killed. We are supposed to hate people—be very tough customers. But as soon as the fighting is over, we Americans begin to feel sorry for the enemy. And it's hard to keep that icy front when people act friendly."

APRIL 3: *Naha, a city in southern Okinawa*

The tall, broad-shouldered General Mitsuru Ushijima sipped from a glass of Scotch whiskey as he listened to one of his officers reporting on the American landings thirty miles away. "Let them land," Ushijima said, "and come to us."

Ushijima said two things would create a "magnificent" Japanese victory. One, the Divine Wind—the kamikazes—would blow up American supply ships off Okinawa's beaches. The Americans on the island would be cut off from food and ammunition. Second, the weakened Americans would be lured to this southern side of the island where Ushijima had 100,000 defenders hidden inside the caves of the rock-ribbed mountain.

His men, said Ushijima, "will be firing down the throats of the Americans." Hundreds, perhaps thousands, of Americans would die for each foot of rock they took on Okinawa. He vowed that the American advance would stall there. It could be the war's last battle. After being bloodied at Okinawa, he said, the Americans would plead for peace talks.

APRIL 5: *Berlin, Hitler's bunker under the garden of the Reich Chancellory*

Hitler was pointing to a map on the clam-gray concrete wall. His arms shook uncontrollably. The map showed that Hitler's Third Reich, once a blanket over Europe, had now shrunk to a square patch no more than 300 miles wide, the Soviets on one side, Eisenhower's armies on the other.

German victory was now at hand, Hitler growled to his generals. The Soviet Army had spread itself so thin over Europe, he muttered, "that the decisive battle can be won in Berlin."

His generals urged him to flee Berlin. No, said Hitler, he would stay in the capital. "I have just decorated a thirteen-year-old boy with the Iron Cross," he said. The boy had blown up a Russian tank. He was one of hundreds of thousands of teenagers and older men, some sixty and older, who had been recruited as a "People's Army." With brave boys like that, he shouted, the battle for Berlin could be won.

He dictated this order to his troops facing the Red Army: "Our mortal enemy—the Jewish Bolshevik—has begun his final massive attack. He hopes to smash Germany and wipe out our people. . . . At this hour Germany looks to you. . . . By your weapons and under your leadership the Bolshevik attack will drown in a batch of blood."

APRIL 6: *Aboard the U.S. destroyer* Newcomb
off Okinawa

The kamikazes swerved in the dusky evening sky, black puffs of smoke nipping at their wingtips. American warships were firing furiously to keep what gunners called a "killing wall" between the planes and the ships.

The *Newcomb* was one of dozens of destroyers code-named "small boys." They were lined up as a "fence" between the big boys—carriers and battleships—on the other side of Okinawa. American commanders hoped that the young kamikaze pilots would be lured to the destroyers and shot down before they attacked the big boys. "We are," a destroyer commander told his crew, "the sacrificial lambs."

Three kamikazes began their dives. Dipping and swerving, they aimed their noses at the *Newcomb*'s port side. Blue and red tracers flew by their wings.

The ear-ringing din on the *Newcomb*'s deck was split by a cheer. A gunner's direct hit blew up a kamikaze—"almost in my face," one gunner said later. But the second kamikaze smashed into the *Newcomb*'s stern. The third knifed deep into the *Newcomb*'s steel flank, crashing to a stop in the engine room. The engine-room sailors stared openmouthed at the red-hot, twisted metal ribs of what had been a plane—but only for a moment. Most were blown into the steel bulkheads of the *Newcomb* as the plane's bomb exploded.

Furnaces erupted, flames shooting upward and blowing gaping holes in the *Newcomb*'s steel-plated deck. One sailor, rising groggily to his feet, climbed a ladder to escape what he later called a "burning pot of rubble."

He staggered onto the main deck and saw that most of the ship was wrapped in orange flame and black smoke.

APRIL 6: *Aboard the destroyer* Leutze *off Okinawa*

*L*eutze's skipper, Lieutenant Leon Grabowski, ordered his ship to come alongside the burning *Newcomb*. Flames singed the hair of *Leutze*'s sailors as they passed fire hoses to the men on the deck of the *Newcomb*.

"Kamikaze! Nine o'clock!"

Grabowski heard the shout amid the ear-splitting noise of blasting guns and roaring kamikaze engines. He saw another bomber, called an Oscar by American gunners, diving straight at the *Newcomb*. The *Newcomb* gunners were still firing as flames turned the steel under their feet a glowing red. A shell caught the Oscar's wing. It spun crazily and crashed into *Leutze*'s fantail, where it blew up.

"Fire in compartments near ammunition," an officer shouted to Grabowski on the bridge. "And we're taking in water near the fire room."

Grabowski ordered the *Leutze* to stay linked to the *Newcomb* by fire hoses. The crews could join together to fight the fires on both ships.

Suddenly the *Leutze* listed sharply, throwing Grabowski against the railing of the bridge.

"Am pulling away," he signaled to the *Newcomb* skipper. "In danger of sinking."

APRIL 6: *Aboard the* Newcomb

Lieutenant Al Capps was being pulled out from under the tail of the wreckage of the kamikaze. One of Capps's legs was shattered, but he waved away a medical corpsman. He picked up a fire hose and hobbled toward a fire, shouting orders for sailors to pull another hose closer to the flames.

Machinist's Mate Richard Tacey was scurrying up a ladder to a main deck when he heard screams from below him. Tacey jumped off the ladder. He saw flames leaping from where the ship's "black gang" of coal stokers fed the furnaces. Tacey ran to a door and pulled it open. Now he could hear shouts coming from the men of the black gang, who were trapped behind a hatch. Black smoke blinded Tacey as he groped with his hands to open the hatch.

It flew open. Two badly burned sailors staggered through the smoke. They left behind the smoking bodies of most of the black gang — and Richard Tacey, dead of smoke suffocation.

APRIL 6: *Aboard the* Leutze

From his bridge, Lieutenant Grabowski could see the tug pulling the smoking *Newcomb* toward a nearby island. The *Leutze* also was being towed across the now dark sea. The fires on both ships had been put out. Corpsmen moved along the blackened deck, giving painkillers to men moaning with scorched bodies.

Grabowski was dictating a report to his

commander: "All crews of guns continued to fire during the attacks until the gunners were killed or blown overboard into the sea."

He had lost twenty of his ninety men. When *Leutze* tied up at a repair dock, he was told that kamikazes had sunk or damaged 24 ships so far today, killing or injuring at least five hundred.

APRIL 7: *Pearl Harbor, Hawaii, Pacific Fleet headquarters*

The war correspondent had seen the worried faces of Admiral Chester Nimitz's staff as teletype machines clacked with reports from Okinawa on damage done by the kamikazes. "For the first time in the fighting in the Pacific," the reporter cabled the *New York Times,* "the morale of the U.S. Navy has been shaken by casualties that were never this high at even Midway or the Coral Sea battles of two or three years ago."

Nimitz told the correspondent that "of all the Japanese weapons of this war, and that includes their giant battleships and carriers and naval air force, the suicide pilots are one of their most effective."

Nimitz paused, then added: "And perhaps their *most* effective."

APRIL 12: *Warm Springs, Georgia*

In one corner, the artist's hand hovered over an easel, finishing a brush stroke. She was painting a portrait of the President, who sat in his wheelchair signing papers. Two of Roosevelt's cousins, Laura Delano and Daisy Suckely, sat nearby. He liked to chat with these two, and another visitor, Lucy Rutherford. He was telling stories of life in Washington that made them smile and, occasionally, blush.

Roosevelt glanced at his watch. The time was 12:45 P.M. "We have fifteen more minutes of work," he said. He held a pen over a document and shouted to the women, grinning, "Here's where I make a law!"

The grin froze on his face. He reached a hand behind him and said, "I have a terrific pain in the back of my head." He slumped forward in the chair.

He never spoke again. He was carried, unconscious, to a bedroom. Three hours later, doctors pronounced him dead, killed by a stroke.

APRIL 12: *Washington, the White House*

Nervously fingering his steel-rimmed spectacles, the vice president of the United States, Harry Truman, walked into a room where Eleanor Roosevelt sat with her daughter. Truman was asking himself why he had been told to hurry to the White House. The President wasn't even here. What was wrong?

"Harry," Eleanor Roosevelt said, "the President is dead."

Truman could not speak for several seconds.

Then, gently, he asked, "Is there anything I can do for you?"

She looked up at him. "Tell us," Eleanor said, "is there anything we can do for you? For you are the one in trouble now."

An hour later Harry Truman stood stiffly in front of a justice of the Supreme Court. At his side were his wife, Bess, and their daughter, Margaret. The justice swore in Harry Truman as the new president of the United States.

APRIL 12: *Near Erfurt, Germany*

Eisenhower's face suddenly turned white as he came within 100 yards of the death camp. The sour, acrid stench made him gasp. Walking with him toward the barbed-wire fences were his two top generals, Omar Bradley and George ("Blood and Guts") Patton, his silver-handled pistol strapped to his side.

His generals had told Eisenhower of the horrors they had seen as American troops smashed across Germany. Their troops had liberated hundreds of thousands of Jews, gypsies, the mentally ill, the old, the helpless—people Hitler had called "inferior." In camps like Buchenwald, Dachau, and Belsen, the generals had talked to the survivors—bony, sunken-cheeked men, women, teenagers, tots as young as one or two. The survivors told of being jammed into cattle cars, taken to camps where gas chambers killed quickly, or where beatings and starvation killed slowly.

As Ike entered the camp, he had to hold a handkerchief to his nose to block out the odors of death. "Even after I had heard the stories of what I should expect to see," he said later, "these awful sights had to be seen to be believed."

He saw more than 3,000 naked corpses piled high against walls. Their wide, glassy eyes seemed to stare at him as if pleading that he should understand how they had suffered. Gaunt men and women gathered around him to

Grim sights like these of caged Jews, Rumanians, gypsies, and other Hitler "undesirables" shocked General Eisenhower and other Americans as the "death camps" were liberated. Eisenhower forced German civilians to walk every inch of each death camp. *(Photo courtesy of the National Archives)*

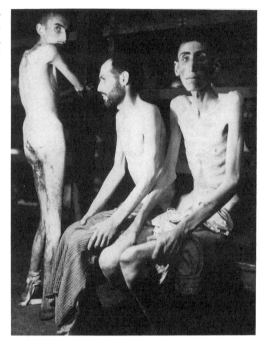

These human skeletons were among the dead and the dying found at the death camps. Some experts estimated that the Holocaust consumed twelve million lives. *(Photo courtesy of the National Archives)*

tell how husbands, wives, fathers, children, even babies were herded into gas chambers. They showed him torture posts where bodies had been torn to shreds by whips of wire. They told of guards pulling weeping children from shrieking mothers. The mothers were killed, the children sent to work as slave laborers.

The horrors he was seeing and hearing were too much for General Patton, who knew the stench of battlefields in two world wars. He left Ike, went to a nearby building, and retched.

Ike told an aide, "I want every American unit not actually at the front to see this place. We are told that the American soldier does not know what he is fighting for. Now, at least, he will know what he is fighting against."

He drove to Patton's Third Army headquarters. Aides told him that millions had died in the death camps—perhaps as many as ten to twelve million, at least half of them Jews.

"I can't understand how the German people could do a thing like that," Ike said to Patton.

"Not all of them can stomach it," said one of Patton's officers. "In one camp we paraded the townspeople through, to let them have a look. The mayor and his wife went home and slashed their wrists."

"Well, that's the most encouraging thing I have heard," Ike said. "It may indicate that some of them still have a few sensitivities left."

APRIL 21: *Near Naha, Okinawa*

"Talk Navajo," one marine said to the marine with a portable radio transmitter strapped to his sweaty back.

The radioman jabbered words into the microphone. "What's he saying?" asked a third marine. "I can't understand a word."

"He's a Navajo Indian," the first marine said, nodding at the radioman. "He talks Navajo lingo to other radiomen who are Navajos. The Japs can't read our messages."

The radioman was relaying orders from the headquarters of General Simon Buckner's Tenth Army. Buckner's 200,000 soldiers and marines now ringed General Ushijima's 100,000 men hiding in the mountains that rose above Naha and the sea.

"The Japs have nowhere to go; let them starve in their caves," a marine general told Buckner.

No, Buckner said. It would take too long to starve out the Japanese.

The Navajo radioman was listening to orders coming from Buckner's headquarters. He put down his earphones.

"This is going to be a slugging match between us and the Japanese in their caves," he said. "Buckner wants to go straight at 'em."

APRIL 22: *Berlin, Hitler's bunker*

His generals stood in a circle around Hitler. He sat in a chair, his legs and arms shaking, his face yellowish.

Two days ago he had ordered the generals to counterattack with two armies to stop the Red Army's drive on Berlin. "Any commanding officer who keeps his men back," he ranted, "will lose his life within five hours!" His firing squads had already killed officers accused of flying to neutral Sweden and Switzerland and making offers to surrender to Eisenhower.

To come to Hitler's bunker, the generals had bounced in their cars on streets filled with rubble and dotted with bomb craters. Stunned Berliners hid in shelters as Allied bombers rained down bombs day and night. The wail of air-raid sirens never ceased. Thousands of Soviet guns zoomed shells that shook the city. Flames gushed from buildings. There were no lights, no heat, no food.

"Berlin is three-quarters surrounded," a general told Hitler. Another said that his troops could not hold back the Red Army for more than a few more days.

Hitler leaped from his chair. He shouted

that he was surrounded by traitors and liars. His left arm flapping wildly, he shrieked that he was being betrayed by cowards.

Suddenly he flopped back into the chair and growled, "The war is lost!"

There was a long silence, the generals too stunned by Hitler's sudden admission of defeat to speak. Finally, one said that Hitler could still slip out of Berlin and escape. No, he said, his voice an unemotional monotone, he would die here in this bunker.

APRIL 25: *Washington, the White House, the Oval Office*

The tall, graying secretary of war, Henry Stimson, faced Harry Truman across the President's desk. Two weeks ago Stimson had whispered to Truman: "I want to speak to you soon about a highly secret matter."

That time had come, Stimson said. He pushed across the desk twenty-four typewritten pages. He asked Truman to read carefully the first sentence: "Within four months we shall in all probability have completed the most terrible weapon ever known in human history, one bomb of which could destroy a whole city."

Stimson told Truman what neither Eisenhower nor MacArthur nor Stalin knew of the new weapon. Indeed, only a handful of men around the world knew of it. At a cost of two billion dollars, thousands of American scientists and technicians—most not knowing what they were working on—had come close to making the world's first atomic bomb.

Truman read the twenty-four-page report. He looked up at Stimson. How, he asked, did the scientists know that the bomb really would wipe out a city?

The bomb would soon be tested in the New Mexico desert, Stimson said. If it worked, Truman would then have to decide if it should be dropped on a Japanese city, killing perhaps as many as a million men, women, and children.

Mrs. Roosevelt had been right, Truman said later. He was the one in trouble now.

APRIL 26: *Strahla, a village on the Elbe River in southern Germany*

U.S. Army Lieutenant Al Kotzebuhue, who could speak Russian, poked his head from the hatch of his armored car. Peering across the river with his binoculars, he saw what looked like Red Army helmets on the other side. Kotzebuhue and his thirty-five-man patrol had been sent ahead by his Third Army commander to try to make contact with Red Army troops coming from the east.

Kotzebuhue jumped out of his armored car. He found an abandoned sailboat. He and three men sailed to the other side of the river.

Soldiers, red stars on their uniforms, pointed rifles as the Americans bobbed toward a pier. Kotzebuhue stood up in the boat and shouted, "Americans . . . we are Americans."

Two men who fought across Europe to cut Hitler's army in half meet in Linz, Austria. Shaking hands and soon to begin swapping souvenirs are an American on the left and a Red Army fighter on the right. *(Photo courtesy of the National Archives)*

Minutes later Kotzebuhue and his men were clinking glasses with Red Army soldiers, and toasting Roosevelt, Truman, and Stalin. Eisenhower's armies had crossed almost half of Europe in the eleven months since D Day to link up with the Red Army coming from the other direction. Eisenhower's armies had paid for their crossing with 425,000 casualties, including 70,000 killed in action.

APRIL 28: *Berlin, Hitler's bunker*

Red Army soldiers now prowled within a few hundred meters of the bunker, an officer told Hitler. An armored car waited in the Chancellory garden, he said. Its crew wanted to fight their way out of the city, carrying Hitler with them.

"We would merely flee from one cauldron to another," Hitler said calmly. "Am I, the Führer, supposed to sleep in an open field or in a farmhouse or something like that, and just wait for the end? No, it would be far better for me to remain here."

He ordered a judge brought to the bunker to marry him and Eva Braun.

APRIL 28: *Milan, Italy*

The message from the British general was handed around the table from one guerrilla commander to another. Each guerrilla—most were members of Italy's Communist Party— shook his head as he read the message from the British general. "No," said one guerrilla chieftain. "Mussolini must die—now!"

The brick-jawed, strutting Benito Mussolini and his Fascist Party had ruled Italy since the 1920s. A former Communist himself, he had jailed and killed Communists, winning the approval of fellow dictator Hitler. He and Hitler had agreed to be what were called the Axis partners. But Mussolini had stayed out of the war until 1940, when he tried to grab North African land away from the weakened French and British. His poorly trained Italian soldiers ran from British tanks and had to be rescued by Hitler's Afrika Korps. When Eisenhower's armies invaded Italy in 1943, Italy's king asked for peace. He put Mussolini in jail. Hitler's troops set him free, but the war's defeats had turned him into a weak and shaky old man.

Mussolini hid out in north Italy with a girlfriend, Claretta Petacci. By now, Allied soldiers had come within a few miles of his hideout. He disguised himself as a German soldier and tried to escape into Germany. A guerrilla recognized him. He was now being held in the nearby town of Dongo.

The British general's message ordered the guerrillas to hold Mussolini for a war crimes trial. But the Italian Communist leader, Palmiro Togliatti, demanded that his Fascist enemy, Mussolini, be killed immediately.

A broad-shouldered, mustached guerrilla, Walter Audisio, was picked to do the killing. He shoved an automatic pistol into his belt, rose, and left for Dongo.

APRIL 28: *Near Dongo, Italy*

M ussolini was sitting with Claretta in the bedroom of a farmhouse, the door guarded by a guerrilla. The door suddenly flew open. Audisio stood at the entrance and shouted, "I have come to rescue you!"

Mussolini was not fooled. "Really," he said sarcastically, knowing Audisio had to be a Communist.

Audisio hurried Mussolini and Claretta into a car. The car rolled a few hundred yards. Audisio ordered it to stop.

He asked Mussolini and Claretta to follow him to the front of a house. At the gate he suddenly wheeled on Mussolini and shouted, "By orders of the general headquarters of the Volunteers for Freedom Corps, I am required to render justice to the Italian people!"

Sweat beaded across the forehead of the nervous Audisio. He aimed the automatic pistol at Mussolini.

"No, he must not die," Claretta cried. She clasped the bald, stout Mussolini around the neck.

"Move away if you don't want to die, too!"
Audisio said nervously.

She stepped aside. Audisio pulled the trigger. Five bullets burst through Mussolini's
body. He fell onto his knees, then pitched,
head-first, onto the ground. Audisio turned to
face Claretta. Another burst killed her instantly.

APRIL 29: *Berlin, Hitler's bunker*

H itler was dictating his will to one of his
secretaries. He told her that he had never
wanted the war to begin. The war, he said in
his raspy voice, had been started by those "of
Jewish origin or [who] worked for Jewish inter-
ests." He had decided to "choose death volun-
tarily" and "die with a joyful heart." He
ordered his commanders not to surrender but
"to set a shining example of faithful devotion to
duty until death."

A few hours earlier he had wed Eva Braun.
Now he finished his last will: "My wife and I
choose to die in order to escape the shame of
overthrow or capitulation. It is our wish that
our bodies be burned immediately."

APRIL 30: *Milan, Italy*

M en, women, and children filled the
streets, staring upward, Some shouted
insults at the dangling bodies. The eyes of others were filled with horror. The bullet-smashed
bodies of Benito Mussolini and Claretta Petacci

had been strung up by their feet. The bodies swung from a girder above a gas station. At this station a year earlier the Germans had executed fifteen guerrillas. Today the guerrillas had taken their revenge.

APRIL 30: *Berlin, Hitler's bunker*

Hitler was saying good-bye to his secretaries and servants. He turned to his pilot, Hans Bauer, and said, "On my tombstone they ought to put these words, 'He was the victim of his generals.' "

Then, his face grim, he mumbled, "I'm ending it today."

At 3:30 P.M. he and Eva Braun Hitler closed the door of their living room. They sat on a couch. Hitler faced a picture of a German emperor, Frederick the Great, and another of his mother.

Two heavy pistols lay nearby. Eva said she wanted to die by poison. "I don't want death to hurt," she had told him earlier. She bit into a small tube filled with poisonous cyanide. Her head fell back, and she slumped over onto the couch.

Hitler bit down on another tube filled with cyanide. Then he put a pistol to his right temple and pulled the trigger. The blast pitched his body against a small table, upsetting a flower vase. Water splashed onto Eva's body.

Hearing the shot, an aide opened the door. He signaled for officers to carry the bodies up the steep stairs of the bunker. They opened a door to the Chancellory garden, then jumped back as a shell exploded.

Red Army guns had zeroed in on the area. One after another, shells tore craters in the chewed-up garden. Two of Hitler's closest aides, Joseph Goebbels and Martin Bormann, crept up the stairs to watch.

The shelling slowed, then ceased. Soldiers lifted the bodies and carried them to a shallow gully in the garden. A soldier poured gasoline onto the bodies. He hurried back to the doorway as an exploding shell shook the ground.

An officer ran to the bodies, lit a gasoline-soaked rag, dropped the burning rag, then scurried for safety. Fire and black smoke curled around the bodies of Eva and Adolf Hitler. The smoke ballooned above the garden. It mixed with the clouds of smoke that hung like a thick brown and black blanket over the shaking, blazing ruins of Hitler's Third Reich.

Chapter Five

MAY 1: *A kamikaze base near Tokyo*

Only five planes could still fly after a month of kamikaze attacks on the American warships clustered around Okinawa. So far the suicide pilots had sunk thirty American warships and damaged almost 350.

Captain Rikihei Inoguchi was asking for volunteers to fly the five remaining planes. Pilots grabbed at his arms and shouted, "Please send me!"

Captain Inoguchi pulled away, screaming: "Everybody wants to go! Don't be so selfish!"

MAY 2: *Near Dachau, Germany*

Sixteen-year-old Sam Pisar and two other teenage Jewish boys were hiding in a thatched-roof hut. They had escaped from the Dachau death camp four days earlier. Their German guards had heard the booming of American guns and fled. The boys had ducked into this hut after seeing German machine gunners set up their guns at a nearby crossroad.

Sam had survived four years of Hitler's

death camps. His mother and father had been gassed to death. He did not know what happened to his brothers and sisters. He had been beaten, starved, and forced to bury dead Jews and other "undesirables" in mass graves.

Sam was munching on a raw potato he had found in a field. It was the most food he had devoured in one sitting in more than three years. His grimy, striped prison uniform flapped on his thin arms and legs.

Sam stopped his hungry munching when he saw the Germans swivel the gun to face the hut. "They saw us," Sam told the other boys.

A loud rumbling shook the hut. Sam peered through a window. A mustard-brown tank lumbered down the road. There was a huge blue star on its side. "My skull," Sam said later, "seemed to burst." Somehow he knew that this was a tank of the United States of America.

Sam bolted out of the hut. "Come back," the other boys shrieked, "they'll kill you."

Machine-gun bullets kicked dirt at his heels as he ran toward the tank. The tank stopped. Its gun belched fire and smoke.

Panting, Sam kept on running. He could hear only his breathing, and realized the machine gun was no longer firing. He looked up and saw the tank's hatch fly open. A soldier, wearing a dark-green helmet, wiggled out of the hatch and dropped to the ground. Sam looked into the brown face of what his teachers had told him was a "Negro American."

Sam fell at the soldier's feet. He threw his arms around the soldier's legs and cried out, "God Bless America!"

MAY 2: *Neubrandenburg, Germany*

Captain Frank Sampson had just been freed by Red Army soldiers from the Stalag II-A prisoner-of-war camp. Captain Sampson, a Catholic chaplain, had been captured by the Germans in December during the Battle of the Bulge.

Sampson stood with a freed French prisoner on a hill overlooking burning Neubrandenburg. Their faces could feel the heat even a mile away as fiery-tongued Soviet rockets rained down into the flames wrapped around the city.

Sampson and the Frenchman decided to go to Neubrandenburg. They wanted to help a German priest who had smuggled food into their prison camp. On the way they saw dozens of bodies of German women and girls, raped and then killed by Red Army soldiers. The throats of some of the women had been slit. Others hung from trees by their ankles.

The stench of burning flesh sickened them as they came close to the city. Hungry former prisoners looted stores for food and clothing. Sampson found the German priest slumped on the steps of his wrecked church. His mother and two sisters had been raped by Soviet soldiers.

Sampson walked sadly back to his old

prison camp. He met a Soviet colonel. He told
the colonel of the savagery by Red Army soldiers. The colonel admitted to Sampson that
Soviet soldiers were leaving a bloody trail of
slaughtered men, women, children, and even
babies as they marched through Germany. "It's
the same bloody trail," the colonel said grimly,
"that Hitler's butchers left in 1942 when they
marched through our Motherland."

MAY 2: *In a British scout plane over Rangoon, Burma*
Commander Albert Saunders swooped his
swift Mosquito over the city. "No Japanese troops seen," he radioed his base. "I'm going to land."

"Be careful," a radio dispatcher told him.
"The Japs are retreating and desperate. They're
killing prisoners."

Saunders turned the plane and began a steep
glide toward Mingladon Airport. He knew that
the British Fourteenth Army had driven close
to Rangoon. The drive had begun early in 1945
as British and Indian troops took off from bases
on the Burma-Indian border. They cut through
jungles, sweating in the 140-degree heat, blasting Japanese forts to bits. Only a handful of Japanese soldiers had been left to guard the forts.
The Japanese were bringing soldiers from
Southeast Asia back to guard the homeland islands against an American invasion.

The Japanese had overrun Southeast Asia in
the first few months of the war. In 1942 Amer-

ican general Joseph ("Vinegar Joe") Stilwell told Roosevelt he could take back Burma with British and Chinese troops. But the British argued against an exhausting jungle war. China's dictator, Chiang Kai-shek, did not want to risk his troops fighting the Japanese. Those troops kept him propped on his throne.

Stilwell wanted to take Burma so that ships from America could dock at its large port, Rangoon. American guns and food could then be trucked to Chiang's seven-million-man army in China. That army, said Stilwell, could pin down more than a million Japanese in China while MacArthur hopped across the Pacific toward the Philippines and Japan.

The hot-headed Stilwell insulted Chiang and was fired by Roosevelt. But Stilwell oversaw the building of the Burma Road. It rollercoasted up and down more than a thousand miles of the world's steepest mountains from India to China. African-American engineering troops built the road, using native labor. African-American GIs were now steering trucks around the hairpin turns of the Burma Road, carting tons of weapons to China. "For every mile of the Burma Road," an engineer said, "there is an American grave."

Saunders landed the Mosquito. He and his five-man crew crept out of the plane, scanning the dusty airfield. They trained their guns on the airport tower—but heard only the whining of the wind.

A man came running toward them. Six guns swung to point at his head. He was, Saunders saw, a Burmese man. "The Japanese gone," he shouted. "Left an hour ago!"

"We took Rangoon single-handed, mates," Saunders said, laughing.

Saunders sent a radio message to General William Slim, whose Fourteenth Army troops had encircled Rangoon: The road into Rangoon was clear. An hour later, British and Indian troops marched into the deserted city.

Using Rangoon as a springboard, Slim said, he would retake Malaya. Free French troops, he said, would sail from Rangoon to blast the Japanese out of prewar French Indochina. But a native leader in the capital, Hanoi, had renamed French Indochina. Ho Chi Minh called it Vietnam and proclaimed its independence.

MAY 3: *On the destroyer* Aaron Ward *off Okinawa*

Lieutenant Commander Arnold Lott, standing high on the ship's bridge, saw it first—a black dot scurrying across the evening sky. Then the kamikaze was diving toward the *Aaron Ward*'s smokestack.

"Range nine 00 double 0," a gunner was shouting. "Range eight 00 double 0 . . . Range seven 00 double 0."

Even from this range of 7,000 yards—about four miles—the gunners could see that the kamikaze was a Val fighter. An egg-shaped bomb hung from its belly.

"Commence firing!"

Five-inch guns boomed. Fiery tracer shells streaked upward in red and white curves.

"Range five 00 double 0."

Lott could see smoke trailing from the Val. Moments later another shell smashed into its nose, and the plane became flying bits of debris showering down on the *Aaron Ward*. The suicide pilot's body soared like a bullet over the heads of the *Ward*'s gunners and smacked into the sea behind them.

Gunner Shorty Abbott looked down from gun mount 53 and saw a crumpled engine smoking at his feet.

"Get it out of here," he yelled.

Sailors tugged at the Val's engine, blistering their hands as they shoved it overboard.

Radarman Glenn Newman, staring at his screen, was calmly speaking by phone to the bridge: "Many bogies . . . many bogies." Then: "Here comes another one."

"All guns action port, action port."

"Commence firing . . . commence firing."

Fingers pressed firing buttons. Tracers flew toward the Val, now a mile and only ten seconds away.

The Val blew up, a ball of red fire that pinwheeled into the ocean.

"Another one splashed!" a gunner shouted. There was a weak cheer from throats of sweltering men who had been standing behind guns under the sun for more than two hours.

A Zeke bomber curled across the darkening sky and began its dive. Commander Lott could see a bomb, "a big mean-looking one," nestled under its wings.

Tracers flew by the Zeke as it dipped and swerved at almost water level. Its nose was aimed at the *Ward*'s blazing port-side guns. The Zeke flew over the wide-eyed faces of *Ward* gunners and crashed into the ship's upper deck. Flames roared upward, turning evening into the whiteness of high noon.

The ship shook, wracked by convulsions. Sailors ran into black smoke, coughing, and stumbled over torn and burning bodies.

The *Aaron Ward* began to spin like a dog chasing its tail. The bomb had blown away control lines to the rudder.

A huge hole gaped in the *Ward*'s belly, just below the water line. Machinist's Mate Pete Peterson ran to a doorway in the engine room and was met by a sheet of flame. A blast of hot air sent him sailing across the room. He hit something hard. He saw only blackness for several seconds or several minutes, he wasn't sure. He arose groggily, limped to a ladder, and climbed to the main deck.

Etched against the leaping flames, he saw men running with hoses, twisted guns, crumpled bodies, and thick smoke. He heard screams, saw blood mixed with oil oozing on the deck.

Peterson saw another engine-room sailor,

Steve Stefani, standing near a railing. As Peterson ran toward Stefani, the deck suddenly began lifting toward the sky. For a moment Peterson was running uphill. Something, he realized, had exploded below. He slid down the buckled deck, grabbed a pipe, and stopped his slide. He looked toward where Stefani had stood. Stefani had vanished. Peterson groped his way to the railing and looked down. He saw Stefani's head bobbing in the ship's wake. Then the head vanished in the smoky murk.

Entire gun crews had vanished with Stefani. Peterson heard a shout—"Ahoy, *Aaron Ward.*" A barge had pulled alongside the *Ward,* which now listed sharply on its port side. "If we go under," Pete thought, "we could pull down that barge with us."

The barge's sailors yanked fire hoses onto the deck of the *Aaron Ward.* The ocean now lapped on its port deck. Exploding shells, ignited by fires, rocketed off the deck into the night sky. The explosions knocked down firefighters. But only the wounded and the dead were being taken off the *Aaron Ward.*

MAY 3: *On an autobahn in southern Germany*

A *Yank* writer had joined this infantry company as it rode in trucks down the superhighway toward Nuremberg, one of the last German cities not yet taken by the Allied armies. The *Yank* writer overheard the following conversation between two dogfaces:

"You know, Willie, I'm scared."

"Are you nuts? The way we're going now, the whole thing will blow over in a couple of weeks. Then you can go back to your wife and tell all your kids what a hero you were."

"That's what I'm scared about, Willie. It's almost over and I'm almost home, and I'm scared that maybe just a lucky shot will get me. And I don't want to die now, Willie, when it's almost over. I don't want to die now. Do you know what I mean?"

"I know what you mean."

MAY 4: *Aboard the* Aaron Ward *off Okinawa*

The time was dawn, and the last fires had been put out. Exhausted sailors collapsed on the blackened deck as a tug pulled the listing destroyer to a nearby cove. There the *Aaron Ward* would bury forty-five of its dead and send forty-nine other badly wounded of its 190-man crew to hospitals. Among those wounded, his hands and arms riddled by shrapnel, was Steve Stefani. He had thrashed in oily, burning water for three hours until he was spotted and pulled aboard. He and the crew of the *Aaron Ward* got this radioed message from Admiral Chester Nimitz, Pacific Fleet commander: "We all admire a ship that can't be licked."

MAY 5: *Plön, Germany, headquarters of Admiral Karl Doenitz*

The tall, balding Doenitz faced General Alfred Jodl across Doenitz's desk. In his last will, Hitler had named Doenitz, the chief of his navy, to succeed him. Doenitz had just asked Jodl to fly to Eisenhower's headquarters and plead for a conditional surrender.

Tell Eisenhower, Doenitz said, that we will surrender to you, but let us keep our guns to fight off the Red Army.

Doenitz knew that the Soviet Army had left a bloody trail across Germany. And, like Hitler, he feared Stalin's brutal revenge on a German army that had slaughtered at least a million Russian civilians during the past four years. Doenitz hoped that Eisenhower would accept his surrender, then allow him to keep on fighting the Red Army for a few more days.

"Those Russian barbarians," Doenitz told Jodl, "will slaughter or enslave our people. The greater your success"—in gaining time from Eisenhower so the Germans could hold off the Red Army—"the greater will be the number of German soldiers and refugees who will find salvation in the west."

MAY 6: *San Francisco, the Fairmont Hotel*

Forty-nine nations had sent delegates to the first meeting of the United Nations. In the lobby one delegate from Costa Rica told a reporter: "It is unfair. The Big Five are making all the decisions about the new U.N. behind the closed doors of their hotel rooms."

The Big Five were the United States, Great Britain, France, the Soviet Union, and China. "They want to veto in the U.N.'s Security Council any decisions made by the smaller nations in the U.N.'s General Assembly," the Costa Rican delegate said.

One delegate from a small nation begged that big and small nations begin to cooperate for world peace.

"Not far from my capital," said the delegate from Luxembourg, "are the graves of American soldiers who fell in the battle of the Ardennes. They and millions of other people fell victim to German Nazi aggression. People around the world will not permit this to happen again."

MAY 6: *Reims, France, Eisenhower's headquarters*

General Jodl sat across a table from the American generals. In a room only a few feet away, Eisenhower waited to hear Jodl's answer to his demand for unconditional surrender—the same demand that Roosevelt had made at Cairo back in 1942.

Jodl said that Germany would surrender on one condition: that the Germans would lay down their arms against Eisenhower but go on fighting for forty-eight hours—until May 8— against the Soviets. "You'll soon be fighting the Russians yourselves," Jodl told the Americans. "Save as many Germans as you can from them."

Major General Kenneth Strong left the room. He walked to Eisenhower's office. He suggested that Ike accept the offer of unconditional surrender on May 8.

A few hours later Jodl signed the surrender

paper. He stood up in a room packed with American, Canadian, British, Soviet, and Free French officers and spoke the last words of Hitler's Third Reich into a microphone: "Generals, with this signature the German people and the German armed forces are, for better or worse, delivered into the victor's hands. . . . In this hour I can only hope that the victor will treat them with generosity."

MAY 7: *Near Alamogordo, New Mexico*

Stars littered the night sky above the desert. The tall, lanky scientist buttoned his jacket in the cool air. He glanced nervously at his watch. The time was a little after 4:30 A.M. He peered once more through binoculars at the twenty-foot-high wooden tower several miles away. One hundred tons of high explosives, TNT, sat in packages atop that tower. An electric signal would blow the TNT high into the night sky at any moment.

Would such a shattering explosion blow away buildings 100 miles beyond the desert? Would it kill or injure people as far away as Los Angeles or San Francisco? And would poisonous radioactive dust, mixed with the TNT, kill people even thousands of miles away?

This test had been set up to find the answers to those questions. For the past four years a band of scientists, many of them refugees from Hitler, had worked to build an atomic bomb. They had just finished building the first bomb, which they named Fat Man. They planned to explode Fat Man here in this desert next month. They calculated that Fat Man could set off a blast equal to that of 100 tons of TNT. Now they were going to find out how much damage 100 tons of TNT, laced with radioactive waste, could do.

The boss of the scientists, the lanky Robert Oppenheimer, looked once more at his watch. It jumped on his wrist as the ground swayed under him. He saw a huge orange ball bloom above the desert. It rose higher than a scout plane flying two miles above the desert.

Within the hour Oppenheimer was getting radioed reports from observers scattered as far as 200 miles away. Windows had shattered in towns fifty miles away, but the TNT explosion had knocked down no buildings. Best of all, it had not spread radioactivity beyond a few hundred yards from the tower.

Oppenheimer had a happy grin on his face. The grin faded as he talked to Italian scientist Enrico Fermi. No one knows, Fermi said dourly, whether the atomic bomb's blast would be the equal of 100 tons of TNT or one million tons of TNT.

"I will take bets," Fermi told Oppenheimer, "on whether Fat Man merely destroys New Mexico or wipes out the whole world."

Oppenheimer did not offer to take the bet.

MAY 8: *Washington, the White House*

Harry Truman was writing to his mother. "This will be a historical day," he wrote.

"At nine o'clock this morning I must make a broadcast to the country, announcing the German surrender."

An hour later he stood in his jaunty, confident way in front of radio microphones and movie-newsreel cameras. He told millions of Americans—the most ever to hear a radio broadcast until now: "This is a solemn but glorious hour. General Eisenhower informs me that the forces of Germany have surrendered to the United Nations."

He reminded Americans that Japan had not surrendered. "If I could give you a single watchword for the coming months," he said, "that word is work, work, and more work. We must work to finish the war. Our victory is only half over."

MAY 8: *Paris, France*

T he two soldiers were sitting in front of the Red Cross club, a favorite hangout for GIs on leave from the front. A Frenchman ran by, shouting, *"La guerre est finie!"*

"The war may be over for you, buddy," a bearded GI growled, "but it's not for me." He was going back to his rifle squad in Germany tomorrow.

They heard singing echoing off buildings. A wave of brown and blue uniformed American, Canadian, French, and British men and women swept toward them. Arms linked and

A sailor expresses all his—and the world's—joy during the V-E Day celebration in New York City. Others accepted the joyous day more quietly: Churches were packed. *(Photo courtesy of the National Archives)*

heads thrown back, the soldiers and sailors were singing, "Show me the way to go home."

"Is it true?" the bearded rifleman asked the military policeman standing at the door of the Red Cross club.

"I keep telling everybody that it's over," the MP said, "but nobody believes me."

MAY 8: *Paris, the 108th General Hospital*

Nurses wheeled patients out onto the balcony to watch the fireworks. Red, white, and blue rockets wiggled across the sky. Fighter planes zoomed above the Champs Élysées. Pilots spotted the hospital's Red Cross markings and flew low, wiggling their wings in salute.

Private Ernest Kuhn had just been freed from a prisoner-of-war camp. He still had shrapnel in his throat. "I listened to the news," he told a visitor, "and I kept saying to myself that I was still alive. The war was over and I was still alive. And I thought of all the boys in my

Residents of a New York City tenement turn their building into a giant waterfall of paper. For the first time since 1942, Americans were filled with excitement about the future. Germany had finally surrendered. *(Photo courtesy of the National Archives)*

division who were with me in the Ardennes who are dead now."

Private Junior Powell told a nurse: "It's a great thing all right, but I kinda wish it all happened a month ago." He pointed to a leg that was no longer there.

MAY 8: *New York City, Times Square*

"Just like New Year's Eve before the war," people shouted to each other. More than 500,000 men and women, Army khaki and Navy blue mixing with civilian browns and grays, stood shoulder to shoulder. They cheered the news of V-E Day flashed by electric bulbs that ribboned around the *Times* building. Confetti fluttered down from windows. Strangers kissed, hugged, smiled into faces often wet with tears, then moved on to kiss and hug other strangers.

As theater marquees' lights blinked on, Mayor La Guardia broadcast an order that Times Square be cleared. "War workers," he said, "should report for midnight shifts."

MAY 8: *Los Angeles, California*

The bedlam of V-E Day came to an end here at about 3:00 P.M. with a proclamation from Mayor Fletcher Bowden. He asked that church bells begin to peal.

"This is a time for prayer that the war in the Pacific will soon be ended and, with it, World War II," he said. "This is not a holiday."

MAY 12: *Near Naha, Okinawa*

Marine Sergeant Ed De Mar stared upward at the hill. It loomed large in the late afternoon's slashing rain—maybe fifty feet high, two or three football fields long. "It looks like a loaf of bread," someone had said, and soon it had won a name: Sugar Loaf Hill.

Marine shells had slammed into Sugar Loaf for much of the day. Sugar Loaf and two nearby hills had been turned into fortresses by the Japanese. Tunnels snaked through the hills, connecting gun platforms. Mounted on the platforms were guns taken from damaged battleships. Their shells could blow away the biggest tanks.

Ed De Mar's riflemen had just been ordered to seize the top of Sugar Loaf. "No one knows what we'll find up there, but we've got to go up," Ed's commanding officer, Lieutenant Dale Bair, told Ed. "We will have four tanks with us. Synchronize your watches for 1600."

Ed gathered his platoon's forty riflemen and machine gunners. Most were eighteen, nineteen, or twenty years old. Ed was twenty-six, the oldest of his company's enlisted men. His riflemen called him "Mom" De Mar. He told them that they would start up the hill within the hour. Each rifleman broke down his M-1 Garand rifle into dozens of metal parts. They carefully cleaned the barrel and oiled the parts. They snapped the parts back into place. They fixed gleaming bayonets to rifle barrels.

At a little after 4:00 P.M.—1600 military

time—De Mar led his marines to the bottom of the hill. They had moved only ten yards when bullets thudded into the dark dirt around them. The slope shook as mortar shells exploded. Hunks of rock ricocheted off helmets, banged into shoulders, peppered the backs of the marines hugging the slope. Balls of fire exploded in front of their faces.

De Mar saw three of his "kids" writhing on the ground. One of the tanks stopped, treads smashed. Another shuddered and toppled into a deep crater.

A third tank leaked smoke from its belly. It stopped. "It's a sitting duck," De Mar shouted. A marine leaped onto the tank and banged at the top hatch with his rifle.

"Get outta there, get outta there, quick," he shouted.

The tank's driver and his gunner scrambled out of the hatch, flopping over the sides. As the driver hit the ground, bullets smashed into his body. De Mar heard him scream, "Mother, Mother, Dad, Dad, please help!" The screaming suddenly stopped.

"If we don't get off here quick," De Mar growled to another sergeant, "there'll be only dead marines on top."

The Japanese gunners were firing from cave mouths only twenty or so feet above De Mar. The marines saw the Japanese muzzles flash. But when the marines aimed bullets at the flashes, the Japanese vanished.

By now their guns had wrecked the fourth

marine tank. Then they popped out from the mouths of other caves, rifles barking.

"We were firing in all directions," De Mar said later, "and also getting it from every direction."

De Mar saw two machine gunners sprawled next to their gun. Lieutenant Bair sprinted by De Mar, grabbed the heavy gun in his bare hands, and sprayed the caves with bullets.

"He's like Superman, standing up there alone, that gun cradled in his arms, shooting away," De Mar was thinking to himself. Suddenly Bair went down, his legs splayed under him, blood spurting onto his green pants and muddy combat boots.

De Mar tried to rise, then fell on his belly as pain bolted through his body. A flying sliver of steel had slashed open his left leg.

Of the forty men who had started up the hill, only four were still alive at the top. And three of those were badly wounded.

De Mar heard someone shouting to him from below: "De Mar, can you crawl?"

"Buddy, I'll crawl all the way to Madison, Connecticut, if I have to!"

"We called for a smoke screen so those of you on top can get down."

Within minutes a curtain of smoke was dropped over the top of the hill. A tank lumbered through the curtain. A corpsman helped De Mar and two other marines scramble onto the top of the tank. As the tank slithered down the hill, De Mar saw blood streaming down the tank's flank. He guessed that the other two marines were bleeding heavily.

At the bottom of the hill a medic lifted De Mar to the ground. "No," De Mar said, "help those other two. They need it more than I do."

The medic shook his head and said, "There's not a chance for either of them."

MAY 13: *Utrecht, Holland*

The gray-haired Leo Stoock watched, his thin face creased with a smile. He was watching American soldiers riding in jeeps through the town. For the first time in five years, Leo Stoock could look a soldier in the face.

A German Jew, Leo had been thrown into one of Hitler's death camps in 1940. His wife and their son, Ernest, had fled to America. Leo escaped from Buchenwald. For four years he posed as a Dutch farmworker. He did odd jobs for farmers during the day. At night he hid in abandoned houses. Whenever a German soldier stared at him, Leo's heart thumped. Each day he had to hope his fake papers would save him.

Two days ago Utrecht had been liberated by the Americans. Leo still kept a safe distance from soldiers. He was watching the Americans from a second-floor window. He saw a soldier leap out of a jeep and run toward him, waving.

"*Kennst Du mich dann nicht, Papa?*" the American soldier was shouting in German.

Leo stared down at the soldier. No, he replied in German, he did not know who the soldier was.

"I'm Ernest, your son!"

Ernest had joined the army in America and returned to Europe as a GI. He had come here after hearing about Jews who had hidden in Utrecht. An hour later he was writing to his mother: "Papa still couldn't grasp it and only when I was inside did he realize I was his son. You can imagine how he kissed me and hugged me then."

MAY 17: *At the bottom of Sugar Loaf Hill, Okinawa*

The marines flopped in the mud, some so tired they slept with eyes open. E Company's 200 men had crawled up the hill four times, reached the top four times, and were driven off four times. Some 160 of E Company's marines were dead, wounded, or missing.

A litter bearer carried a canvas-covered body toward a truck. "He was a good guy," somebody said as the body went by.

"They were all good guys," a sergeant said, staring at the bodies stacked on the truck.

MAY 21: *Long Beach, California*

"The War Department was sure he was dead," the blond woman was telling the Associated Press reporter outside the courthouse. "I received word from the War Department reporting him missing, and last October I was informed he was dead."

Helen Coad-MacDowell was speaking of her first husband, bomber pilot Lieutenant Harold Coad. He had been shot down in a plane over Burma. Six months later she married Navy Ensign Robert MacDowell. Yesterday the War Department informed her that Lieutenant Coad was alive in a Burma hospital.

"Just who is my husband?" she was asking the reporter. "Which one is legally mine?"

A little later, inside a courtroom, a judge told her that she was legally married only to Lieutenant Coad. But she could divorce Lieutenant Coad and marry Ensign MacDowell.

"I am very happy Harold is alive," she told the judge, "but I don't know what to do because I don't want to hurt Mac."

MAY 22: *Atop Sugar Loaf Hill, Okinawa*

Marine riflemen crouched in shallow foxholes. Smoke billowed from caves where Japanese snipers had been burned alive by marine flamethrowers. From nearby slopes the riflemen could hear the rattle of machine guns as other marines from the Second Battalion turned caves into crypts.

American flags waved on Sugar Loaf. The hill had cost the marines more than 2,600 dead and wounded. Another 1,200 had trudged wearily to the rear, too shaken to pull a trigger or hurl a grenade.

"Every man has his breaking point," wrote one marine correspondent. "You can hear just so many shells, see just so many torn bodies, soak just so much rain, spend just so many sleepless nights. And then your irritability turns into silence, your silence into stupor. And then your mouth opens and you scream."

MAY 23: *Lueneberg, Germany, a British prisoner-of-war camp*

Sergeant Major Edward Austin was interviewing German soldiers. Austin, who spoke German, had been ordered to find Hitler's henchmen. Of Hitler's three top Nazis, one was dead and one had been captured. Propaganda Minister Joseph Goebbels had swallowed poison in Hitler's bunker. Air Force Chief Hermann Goering had tried to hide in the hills of southern Germany. But he had stuck up his hands in panicky surrender when American GIs pointed rifles at him. Goering would be tried with other Nazis, General Eisenhower had announced, for "war crimes against humanity."

"The worst of Hitler's henchmen is still missing," Sergeant Austin had been told by a captain. "The worst": Secret Police (SS) Chief Heinrich Himmler. His Gestapo killers wore a death's-head insignia on their caps. They had tortured and killed hundreds of thousands in every country occupied by the German army.

Sergeant Austin had studied pictures of

Himmler. When the next bearded, ragged prisoner entered the room to be questioned, Austin knew right away who he was.

"You are Himmler," Austin growled.

"He doesn't know who I am," Himmler muttered in German to a British officer.

Austin called for a doctor. He suspected that Himmler might be hiding poison to kill himself.

The doctor asked Himmler to open his mouth. He saw something and reached for it with his finger. Himmler bit down on the doctor's finger, crushing a small tube of poison. He fell over, dying within minutes.

MAY 25: *Near Naha, Okinawa*

A marine was writing home. "Mud clings to everything," he wrote. "Food, clothes, guns. Mud in your C rations, mud in your ears. You blow your nose and you blow mud. You keep your rifle close to your body, but how long could you keep it dry? If there was a common prayer, then it was, Don't let me get wounded in the mud. Don't let me get killed in the mud."

More than 65,000 Japanese soldiers and civilians—farmers and their families trapped on the killing fields—had died in that mud. So had some 5,600 Americans. Another 23,000 had been wounded or were missing—the longest American casualty list for any one battle in the Pacific war.

Chapter Six

Salzburg, Austria

The five-foot-six-inch, 125-pound lieutenant looked like a boy as he stood in the ranks of soldiers. The cheeks of his soft, round face glowed red with embarrassment as a general stopped in front of him. Audie Murphy hated to have everyone looking at him.

"Lieutenant Audie Murphy," the general said, reading from a thick sheet of paper, "for exceptional . . ."

The square-shouldered, tight-lipped Audie stood stiffly at attention. He had won medals while fighting in North Africa, Italy, France, and Germany. But now he was about to get the biggest medal of them all.

The general read from a report. It told how Audie had stood on a burning tank destroyer and fought off fifty advancing Germans, saving his men from death.

The general pinned on Audie's chest the nation's highest award, the Congressional Medal of Honor. The general saluted Audie. He had won more medals than any American soldier of World War II.

JUNE 3: *Okinawa, a hill near Sugar Loaf Hill*

Navy medic Bob Rhodes could hear the Japanese snipers shouting at each other from their caves. He was climbing up a rocky slope overlooking the sea. He saw a thin line of marines, fifty feet ahead of him, spraying bullets and flames into the caves. A marine fell. Bob ran to his side, gripping his first-aid kit.

A bullet whizzed by. Hugging the ground, Bob tied a bandage around the marine's arm to stop the spurting blood. He pulled the man into a cave, then gave him sulfa pills.

He heard a moan. He stuck his head out of the cave. He saw another wounded marine. He dragged him into the cave. As he treated the marine's wounds, he heard a shrill shout: "Hey, doc, come on out!"

An English-speaking Japanese sniper had seen the red cross on his sleeve and guessed that he was a doctor.

Bob peered around a rock and saw a bleeding marine hobbling down the slope. He had to let the marine know that medical help was close by.

"Okay, sucker," Bob yelled toward the sniper's position, "I'm coming!"

Head down, Bob ran toward the marine, grabbed him by the waist, and tugged him toward the cave. The sniper's bullets whined by them. Bob and the marine toppled into the cave, now filled wall to wall.

"I dare you to come out of there once more," the sniper shouted.

Bob kept quiet until he saw another marine staggering down the slope. He told himself that by telling the sniper he was coming out, he made the sniper overanxious.

"Get ready!" Bob shouted. "Here I come!"

He leaped sideways out of the cave. He zigged and zagged to the staggering marine. The sniper missed with three shots as Bob tugged his fourth patient into the cave.

"If you come out again, I'll hit you right between the eyes," the sniper shouted.

"Don't go out again, medic," one of the wounded marines told Bob. "He'll get you this time."

Bob crawled to the mouth of the cave. He called to the sniper: "You couldn't hit me if I ran down the barrel of your rifle!"

That dare, figured Bob, should make him even more overanxious. Bob saw another marine bleeding behind a boulder. Bob dashed out of the cave. One bullet zipped by his shoulder, another kicked at his shoe tops. His chest heaving, sweat streaming down his face, Bob pulled the marine toward the cave. Four more bullets flew by him. A fifth hit a rock above his head as he and the marine fell into the cave.

He patched up the fifth marine. The other marines begged him not to go out again. But when Bob looked, he saw two more marines sprawled on rocks.

Suddenly, from behind him, he heard the dry rattle of a Browning Automatic Rifle. Two

JUNE ★ 1945 _____ 119

BAR men had crept up above Bob's cave, spotted the sniper, and silenced him forever.

Bob ran out to give first aid to the two wounded men. Minutes later he and the seven wounded marines arrived at a medical station at the bottom of the hill. "We're alive because of you," one marine said to Bob.

Bob thanked the man, but, silently, he also thanked the bad aim of a boastful sniper.

JUNE 6: *San Francisco, California*

The delegates to the first United Nations conference approved the following preamble to what they called "The New World Charter": "We the peoples of the United States are determined to save succeeding generations from the carnage of war . . . to practice tolerance and live together in peace with one another as good neighbors."

JUNE 7: *Tokyo*

The Japanese education minister, Kozo Ota, told radio listeners that Okinawa's Japanese high school students "are now taking part in the fierce hand-to-hand battles in which American troops were killed by hand grenades.

"Despite fierce artillery fire in the capital city of Naha," he reported, "many students in the upper middle school grades are carrying messages and building fortifications. Girl students are nursing the wounded. Many of the students have died gloriously."

JUNE 15: *New York City*

N oontime crowds stood in the bright sunshine, filling the sidewalks as they watched 200 jeeps roll down Fifth Avenue. In each jeep sat three or four soldiers, sailors, or marines. Some wore bandages around their heads. Some of the men were armless. Others had only one leg. A few had none.

This was the first Purple Heart parade. New York City was honoring men and women wounded during the war. Each jeep carried a sign to tell more than a million spectators where the men had been wounded. The signs passed by with names like Bataan, Kasserine Pass, Midway, Cassino, Leyte, and Okinawa.

New York Times reporter Lucy Greenbaum stood among the spectators. She wrote for the next day's paper: "The crowd . . . was too deeply moved to cheer. Only spasmodic bursts of applause politely pattered from the reviewing stand. The unusual silence persisted — the

Thousands of returning GIs, like this one, overseas for more than forty months were greeted by sons and daughters they had never seen. *(Photo courtesy of the National Archives)*

only sounds the grinding gears of the jeeps—
for the 30-minute parade."

JUNE 15: *Tokyo*

S peaking to the nation on the radio, Premier
Kantarō Suzuki announced that Okinawa
was lost. The Americans, he said, now stood
on the doorstep of Japan. When the Americans
tried to land on Japan's islands, he said, "millions of them were doomed to die.

JUNE 15: *Washington, the Office of Price*
Administration

"D on't you know there's a war on?"
OPA Chief Chester Bowles was re-
peating to reporters those words, so familiar to
Americans over the past four years. The reporters had asked when Americans could find in
stores the things that had been as scarce as gold
for the past four years: sugar, shoes, and gas.

"Not until we win in the Pacific," Bowles
said. Most Americans would still have to get by
with only two pairs of new shoes a year, five
pounds of sugar every four months, and four
gallons of gas a week.

What's more, civilians would have to prove
"this trip is necessary" to buy a ticket on a
train. Railroad cars were badly needed to cart
troops across the country. The troops, coming
from Europe, had to be taken from East Coast
docks to West Coast docks. From there they
would sail to invade Japan.

By 1945 there was an acute shortage of labor; teenage boys and girls became apprentices in a variety of jobs. *(Photo courtesy of the Library of Congress)*

As a result, said Bowles, there would be no baseball All-Star Game this July. Too many people wanted to travel to see the game. "We need train seats for soldiers," he said, "not baseball fans." In fact, he added, the 1945 World Series might also be called off if the two teams were in cities as far apart as Chicago and New York.

JUNE 18: *Washington, the War Department*

More than fourteen million American and European soldiers and sailors were killed in Europe since the war began in 1939, an official told reporters. That number did not include men, women, and children killed in air raids or in death camps.

Total military and civilian casualties in the six-year war in Europe—killed, wounded, missing in action—totaled sixty million. That was the highest toll of any war in history.

JUNE 18: *Washington, the White House, the Oval Office*

P resident Truman told General Marshall and his other war planners that he had just finished reading the 400-page report on Operation Olympic. The report gave the details of the invasion of Japan. The Navy would land 750,000 soldiers, sailors, and marines on one of the Japanese main islands, Kyushu, no later than November 1.

Olympic's planners told Truman that the Americans would be hammered by at least 5,000 suicide planes. The invaders would face more than five million Japanese soldiers and armed civilians. The fighting would be bloodier than on Oki-

The shortage of sugar had become so severe by 1945 that bottles of Pepsi-Cola and Coca-Cola virtually disappeared from store shelves. Parents and their children fill out forms to obtain their regular rations of sugar, sometimes as small as a pound per month. *(Photo courtesy of the Library of Congress)*

nawa. The islands of Japan could be conquered, only after at least a year of fighting and one million American casualties.

Truman winced. Americans, he knew, had been shocked by the death toll on Okinawa. Fathers and mothers were asking why more of their sons were being killed in the Pacific in 1945, while winning battles, than were lost during the defeats of 1942.

His face somber, Truman put down the report and said he would approve Operation Olympic.

"I agree that there is no other choice," Secretary of War Henry Stimson said.

His assistant, John McCloy, asked to speak. He said he thought an invasion of Japan was wrong. "Why not use the atomic bomb?"

Truman listened as McCloy argued that perhaps as many as a million American lives could be saved if Truman dropped what they called "the gadget"—the atomic bomb. Wipe out one city with the gadget, said McCloy, and the Japanese will quickly agree to surrender.

But the atomic bomb is not yet a threat, one planner said. "No one in this room knows whether the gadget really will work."

It will be tested sometime in the middle of July, Stimson said.

If the gadget really worked, Truman said, he might postpone the invasion.

Stimson hurried from the room. He called Los Alamos and told the scientists to make sure that their gadget was tested no later than the middle of July.

JUNE 18: *A hill near Naha, Okinawa*

The burly, barrel-chested General Simon Buckner had come here to watch his Tenth Army soldiers and marines shooting tongues of flame into caves. This operation was called a "mopping up" of the last Japanese holdouts on the island.

A gun boomed from a hill where Japanese gunners were firing at marines. The shell whizzed over Buckner's head and smashed into a slope behind him. Splinters of coral rock flew through the air. One splinter sliced across Buckner's chest. He fell, blood leaping from the wound. Minutes later he was dead.

JUNE 20: *In a B-29 5,000 feet over Wakayama, Japan*

"Bombs away!" the bombardier yelled. The B-29's crewmen stared down at sheets of red and orange flame that shot up from the city. The B-29 was bouncing wildly.

"The air is so hot it's shooting updrafts at us," the pilot, Major Bob Langdale, told the crew in his Texas drawl.

"Look out!" a tail gunner yelled. "The bombs are coming back up at us."

Langdale could see sticks of incendiary bombs, just dropped by his B-29, floating upward in the bubbly hot air. One stick slapped against the belly of the B-29 and exploded, tearing open the bomb-bay door. Another stick blew a hole in the plane's huge fin. The B-29 shuddered, then turned belly-up, flying upside down.

The bombardier, Lieutenant Lou Avrami,

had been staring down at the fires. Suddenly he was seeing only sky, moon, and stars.

Major Langdale pulled hard on the control wheel. Slowly the elephantlike plane turned so that it was flying as it was supposed to fly—its belly down.

"For a moment," Avrami said later, "when I didn't know whether I was looking down at the sky or up at the ground, I wondered if I was dead."

JUNE 22: *Tokyo, the Emperor's Imperial Library*

Seated on his throne in the narrow conference room, Emperor Hirohito—his dainty feet barely touching the floor—listened as a general told him that MacArthur was building an invasion armada on Okinawa and in Manila Bay. More than 1,000 ships and a million men, Japanese spies were telling Tokyo, would sail for Japan no later than November 1.

From a window Hirohito could see flames licking at rooftops after last night's air raid. B-29s sailed over Japanese cities from morning to midnight. Millions of women and children had fled the cities. They left behind at least 200,000 dead.

Hirohito asked about a special messenger he had sent to Moscow. Tell our envoy in Moscow, Hirohito told his foreign minister, to ask the Russians for a favor. Could they bring the Americans to a table for peace talks?

JUNE 22: *A cave in south Okinawa*

In the darkness General Mitsuru Ushijima watched the moon set over the ocean. He could hear the rattle of machine guns and the barking sounds of grenades only a few hundred yards away.

A few hours ago, he had ordered the 10,000 Japanese soldiers and 100,000 civilians still alive on Okinawa to kill themselves. Ushijima and his chief of staff, General Isamu Cho, were preparing to die by hara-kiri.

Ushijima knelt down on a white cloth, facing north toward Tokyo and the Emperor. He

The wreckage of war. Smashed machines are strewn along the beach at Okinawa as the walking wounded are led to a hospital. The Navy lost more ships at Okinawa than at any battle in its history. *(Photo courtesy of the National Archives)*

drove a dagger into his belly and collapsed on the rug. An officer swung a sword and cut off his head.

The battle for Okinawa had ended. Some 200,000 Americans had killed more than 100,000 of Ushijima's defenders. Almost 10,000 had surrendered, by far the most Japanese to surrender since the war began. More than 40,000 Japanese civilians, caught in cross fires of bombings, had been killed: 60,000 were injured.

The cost to America had been the heaviest of all the battles in the Pacific. More than 7,000 soldiers and marines were dead, another 31,000 wounded.

The Navy endured the worst savaging in its history. Nine hundred Japanese pilots had flung their machines onto the decks of warships to kill 5,000 officers and sailors and injure another 4,800. The kamikazes sank ten destroyers, a small carrier, and twenty-five other warships. Damaged were 368 other men-of-war. They included twelve carriers, ten battleships, and five cruisers.

But the American flag had been carried across the Pacific from Pearl Harbor to Okinawa—a distance that was more than twice the size of the United States. The flag now waved within 350 miles of Japan.

JUNE 26: *San Francisco War Memorial Opera House*

One by one, in a long line, the delegates from fifty nations filed onto the stage to sign the Charter of the United Nations. The Charter gave the rules for a new world organization, made up of a Security Council and a General Assembly.

After the last delegate, the one from America, signed, President Truman began to speak to the 3,000 people who filled the Opera House and to millions listening on radio. He said that if the world failed to use the Charter, "we shall betray all those who have died in order that we might meet in freedom and safety to create it."

He suddenly looked up from the typewritten words he was reading. He stared out at the crowd, eyes glittering behind his spectacles. What he really wanted to say, he said, "are the words in my heart—oh, what a great day this can be in history!"

JUNE 30: *Motobu Peninsula, Okinawa*

A marine was writing the latest chapter in the history of the Marine First Division. It had fought longer than any other division in the Pacific Theater. He wrote how the 20,000 marines had been looking forward, after the fighting on Okinawa, to "R and R"—rest and recreation—in Hawaii. Instead they were training to come ashore on the beaches of Japan.

"It had been nearly two years since some of the men had tasted a civilian environment," he wrote. They yearned "to flick a light switch, read road signs, watch children at play, drink a cold glass of milk." Instead, he wrote, "we are expected to fight in the streets of Tokyo."

Chapter Seven

JULY 5: *Washington, Capitol Hill*

"Too many teenagers," one senator said, "are being underpaid, working for only forty or forty-five cents an hour. They could buy an ice cream cone for a nickel before the war. Now the same ice cream costs fifteen or twenty cents."

Leaders of the Congress agreed to debate bills that would raise the minimum wage from forty cents to sixty-five cents an hour.

JULY 8: *Detroit, Ford's River Rouge Plant*

Grinning workers let out a cheer as they faced the newsreel cameras. They were opening a door to show a gray, two-door car rolling out of the factory. This was the first passenger car made in a U.S. factory since 1942. A new 1941 car had cost about $1,000, a Ford official reminded reporters. The new 1946 cars, he said, "will cost at least $2,000."

JULY 16: *Alamogordo Air Base, New Mexico*

The lanky scientist, Robert Oppenheimer, gripped a wooden beam that ran across the top of the shelter. The time was a little after 5:30 A.M., the sky a dirty gray over the desert. Oppenheimer was one of hundreds of scientists, technicians, and soldiers hiding inside shelters. They were waiting for the test of Fat Man, "the gadget" that was either a dud or history's most terrifying weapon of war.

High school students admire posters created by fellow students to spur the sale of war bonds. By 1945 many high schools were filled with sailors and soldiers who had come home to attend graduation ceremonies of younger students before going back to war. *(Photo courtesy of the Library of Congress)*

Fat Man was set atop a 100-foot tower at Ground Zero twelve miles from where Oppenheimer stood. He and other scientists had argued for days. Would Fat Man do what the TNT explosion had not done last month? Would the bomb blow poisonous radioactive clouds toward cities thousands of miles away? Or would Fat Man be a flop? Would what had worked in a lab—a nuclear reaction—work inside a real bomb? Oppenheimer had bet ten dollars with another scientist that Fat Man would be a dud.

A siren wailed. A rocket shot a trail of green light across the sky. Oppenheimer pulled on dark glasses.

"Zero!" A technician's shrill cry blared over

hundreds of loudspeakers across the desert. Fingers pressed buttons; electric impulses jumped through wires plugged into Fat Man.

Oppenheimer stared through his glasses toward Ground Zero. He saw a light as brilliant, one scientist said later, as a "thousand suns."

A yellowish ball of flame swelled above Ground Zero. Within seconds the yellowish ball had risen higher than the Empire State Building. The ball's color changed to blood red. Its top flattened like the top of a mushroom. Night on the desert had suddenly changed into high noon.

Oppenheimer stared at the fiery spectacle. Someone was hugging him and shouting, "Oppie, give me ten dollars!"

Waves of hot air—Fat Man's scalding heat waves—stung Oppenheimer's face. Italian scientist Enrico Fermi had just measured the speed of the heat waves, then done some quick figuring. Fat Man had blown up with a blast equal to an explosion of 10,000 tons of TNT. That was ten times the force of the blast last month that had shattered windows in cities fifty miles away.

An hour later Oppenheimer and Fermi were listening to reports of others who had witnessed the first atomic explosion: "Dazed, awed . . . somehow both pleased and terrified."

"Suddenly there was an enormous flash of light, the brightest I have ever seen or that I think anyone has ever seen. . . . It lasted about two seconds. . . . There was an enormous ball of fire which grew and grew."

"I thought the explosion might set fire to the atmosphere and thus finish the earth."

"The thing that got me was the blinding heat on your face. . . . It was like opening a hot oven."

"While we watched the gray smoke grow into a taller and taller twisting column [the] silence [was] broken after a minute or so . . . by a bang like the crack of five antiaircraft guns going off a hundred yards from you."

"Have we done the work of God or of the devil? A foul but awesome display."

Oppenheimer and Brigadier General Tom Farrell met with the tall, graying General Leslie Groves. He had commanded the secret Manhattan Project that had built this weapon of "God or of the devil."

"The war is over," Farrell said to Groves.

"Yes," said Groves. "After we drop two bombs on Japan."

JULY 16: *Moscow, the Kremlin*

The black-haired, suave Japanese special messenger, Naosoke Sato, bowed as he entered the room. The Soviet diplomat bowed, but just barely.

Sato handed the diplomat a message from his emperor. It was "His Majesty's heart's desire," the message read, "to see the swift termination of the war." Could the Soviets bring America to peace talks with Japan?

The diplomat told Sato he would show the message to Foreign Minister Molotov, who was in Berlin. He showed Sato to the door.

Sato had not been fooled. The Soviets, he told himself as he rode back to his embassy, would not ask the Americans to end the war. The Soviets wanted to jump into the war against a beaten Japan. A defeated Japan would have to give up territory to the greedy Stalin.

Sato radioed the following message by code to Tokyo: "If our country desires to terminate the war, we must accept unconditional surrender."

JULY 18: *Babelsberg, a suburb of Berlin*

President Harry Truman was writing a letter to his mother. He was living in a house here during his talks in nearby Potsdam with England's Prime Minister Churchill and the Soviet's Stalin.

He had flown here, he told his mother, to get Stalin to throw Soviet might against the Japanese. But a secret message, flashed from Alamogordo, had told him that "the gadget" worked. He would not need the Red Army.

"Stalin has thrown up a wall between us and eastern Europe," Churchill told Truman between their meetings with Stalin at Potsdam.

Finishing his letter, Truman wrote of Stalin's rule by terror of Russia and all of eastern

Europe: "A few top hands use clubs, pistols and concentration camps to rule the people." Stalin, he suspected, wanted to spread that rule over the rest of Europe and maybe the world.

JULY 20: *Tokyo, Imperial General Staff headquarters*

"We are estimating that the Americans will land no later than November first on Kyushu," an intelligence officer was telling the assembled generals and admirals. "Operation Ketsu-Go will go into effect as the Americans come ashore."

The battle for Japan, he said, would be won or lost on the beaches. "We must kill as many men as possible and break American morale," he said. Then, he added, the Americans would be forced to come to peace talks. "Bloody the Americans," he said, "and Japan will get the best possible terms in return for surrendering."

More than two million Japanese soldiers and sailors stood on the beaches, he said. Another two and a half million men and women stood behind them. All had sworn to take one American life before dying.

JULY 24: *Babelsberg, a suburb of Berlin*

The wiry, balding Truman scanned the paper handed to him by Secretary of War Henry Stimson. The paper had come from Navy code breakers. They could read every secret message sent by the Japanese. Truman was reading Ambassador Sato's message. He now knew the Japanese wanted to surrender.

He and Stimson came to a decision: They would drop "the gadget" on a Japanese city. But first they would ask the Japanese to surrender. Truman would warn them that their cities could be wiped out. But he would not tell them that the United States was about to drop something as awesome as an atom bomb. "If the bomb fizzles," an adviser told Truman, "we will look like fools."

JULY 24: *Washington, the Pentagon*

Total Army and Navy casualties in World War II now totaled over one million — 1,058,842, an official announced. Almost one in four, about 251,000, had been killed in action. Of the 569,000 wounded so far, said the official, almost three of every five were now fit enough to go back to active duty.

JULY 26: *Potsdam, Germany*

"You can put it on the radio and broadcast it to the Japanese," Truman ordered. He called it the Potsdam Declaration. It demanded that the Japanese surrender unconditionally.

If the Japanese "do not accept our terms," the declaration warned, "they may expect a rain of ruin from the air the likes of which have never been seen on this earth."

Truman knew that the Japanese would think he was threatening only more firebombings.

But his advisers again had warned against mentioning an atomic bomb.

He could sleep at night after ordering the mass killing of men, women, and children, he told Stimson. A few days ago he had seen a photo in *Life* magazine of a Japanese soldier beheading an American prisoner. The photo had been taken from the pocket of a dead Japanese soldier.

One of Truman's aides, Harold ("Chip") Bohlen, said a little later: "The spirit of mercy for the Japanese was not throbbing in our breasts."

JULY 26: *London, 10 Downing Street*

A small crowd had gathered in the warm evening's dusk. A cheer rose as the familiar barrel-like figure of Winston Churchill stepped out the door of the Prime Minister's residence. The pudgy face looked grim, but Churchill threw up his right hand to the crowd. Two fingers formed the V-for-Victory sign that he had made famous during the war.

Today, however, Churchill was a loser. His Conservative Party had been defeated by the Labor Party in a national election. Churchill was on his way to the king's palace to resign; his successor would be the Labor Party's Clement Attlee.

An American reporter asked a man in the crowd: "Why did England vote against the man who led you to victory in the war?"

"Because the Conservatives are for the rich,

the Labor for the working man," the man said. "We trusted Churchill to win a war. But I wouldn't trust him to make sure I had a job after a war."

JULY 28: *Tokyo, the office of the Premier*

R eporters and photographers gathered respectfully in the large room and awaited the arrival of Premier Kantarō Suzuki. He was meeting with his cabinet.

A door opened. Suzuki entered and stood in front of radio microphones. He said that the cabinet had studied President Truman's Potsdam Declaration. He said that the declaration made no mention of the Emperor and his divine right to rule Japan.

Suzuki wanted to say he would "withhold comment" on the declaration. But he forgot to use the words "withhold comment." Instead, referring to the declaration, he used the word *mokusatsu,* which means "ignore."

A radio reporter for Domei, the chief news agency of Japan, began his broadcast to the United States: "Japan will ignore the Potsdam Declaration."

JULY 28: *New York City, atop the Empire State Building*

A rmy Lieutenant Allen Alman and his wife, Betty, peered into the fog that had wrapped itself around Manhattan's skyscrapers. The Almans were standing on the 102nd observatory floor. "This is visibility zero," Alman, an army pilot, told Betty.

Seconds later Alman heard the drone of a plane. He wondered why the plane would be flying so low.

Moments later Alman and his wife were hurtling across the concrete floor. Something had struck the building so hard the floor was shaking. As Alman rose to his feet, he guessed the "something" had to be a plane.

A two-engined B-25 bomber had smashed its nose into the seventy-ninth floor. Women typists ran screaming for doors as flames boiled upward behind them. Oily black smoke blinded the women. Some fell to the floor, eyes and throat stinging. The flames roared over fallen bodies.

An elevator operator opened the door of her car just as the engines of the bomber, its nose now stuck into the side of the skyscraper, exploded. The force blew her into a burning hall. A woman slapped out the flames. She put the operator into the elevator to take her down to the street floor. She could hear sirens screaming in the streets below.

She shut the elevator door, then turned a lever to start the elevator downward. She heard a loud crack. The heat had snapped a cable. The elevator plunged seventy-five floors and crashed into the basement. Rescue workers smashed through walls to get inside the elevator. Hours later they pulled the two women from the wreckage. Their legs were broken, but the women's lives had been saved by a brake that had slowed the elevator's fall.

A pudgy Mayor Fiorello La Guardia huffed and puffed up to the seventy-fifth floor to comfort victims. Thirteen people were dead and twenty-six injured. Among the dead was the B-25's pilot. He had made a wrong turn while flying blind in the fog.

JULY 28: *Potsdam, Germany*

"The Japanese said they will ignore the declaration," Truman was told.

Truman knew that the scientists had shipped an atomic bomb, like the one tested at Alamogordo, to Guam in the Pacific. An Air Corps crew in a B-29 was training to drop the bomb on one of three Japanese cities.

The drop, Truman said, should proceed as scheduled. "That night," he later told his mother, "I had no trouble sleeping."

JULY 29: *Aboard the cruiser* Indianapolis *in the Pacific about 600 miles from Guam*

Captain Charley McVay, the skipper, was asleep in his cabin near the ship's top deck. The *Indianapolis* knifed through the humid air of the tropics. Most of its crew of about 1,000 men tossed belowdecks in their sweaty cots.

At about ten minutes before midnight, a sudden shudder swept through the ship. McVay rose from his cot. Something, he told himself, had hit the *Indianapolis*. A kamikaze, he guessed, but then realized he was too far from shore to be struck by a kamikaze.

He felt the deck shaking under his feet. Suddenly he was sliding on his back across the cabin. White smoke seeped under the door.

He rose groggily and threw open the door. Flames licked upward from a lower deck. An officer told him a submarine had plunged two torpedoes into the waist of the 1,000-foot-long cruiser. McVay felt the ship lurching onto her side. He saw that the bow was dipping deeper into the high, whitecapped waves.

"Have you gotten word from the radio room yet on whether they've gotten off a message?" he asked an officer.

"No sir, not yet."

"Send a message saying we have been hit, give our latitude and longitude, say we are sinking rapidly, and need immediate assistance."

Radioman Larry Woods was already tapping SOS distress signals on his radio's keys. The ship, on its way to the Philippines, had kept its radio silent so signals would not be picked up by Japanese subs known to be nearby. The *Indianapolis* was not due in the Philippines for thirty-six hours. No one would know that it was missing if someone did not pick up Woods's distress calls. But Woods, watching dials, guessed that the explosions had wrecked his transmitter. The radio was dead.

Captain McVay had gone to the bridge. Looking down, he could see smashed bodies of sailors flopped around two jagged holes in the deck below him. Spiraling columns of flame shot from the holes. The flames turned the steel decks white hot, sizzling the bare skin of men too hurt to move. Sailors draped life jackets around the injured, despite their agonized screams: "Don't touch me! Don't touch me!"

"The bow is down below water," an officer told McVay. "I think we are finished. I recommend we abandon ship."

"Okay, pass the word to abandon ship."

McVay started down a ladder. The ship lurched sharply. She was now almost on her port side.

Waves lapped up toward him. Moments later—twelve minutes after being tossed out of his cot—McVay thrashed wildly in the midnight darkness of the Pacific. Waves of oily water flooded his throat and lungs, stinging his eyes.

He looked up, half blinded, and saw his 10,000-ton ship looming above him like a skyscraper. The *Indianapolis* was standing for a moment on her bow, her hull like a fist aiming at the stars. She'll topple over onto me and hammer me to the bottom, McVay thought.

A huge wave washed over him, burying him under the water. When he bobbed upward, he saw the *Indianapolis* knife straight down and suddenly vanish.

A raft was sailing toward him. He grabbed a rope dangling from the raft and clambered on top. He saw a sailor's pale face loom in the darkness. A wave tossed the sailor high above him. "You can make it!" the Captain shouted, reaching out a hand to eighteen-year-old Seaman Ralph Klapper.

"I can't do anything," Klapper gasped, slipping beneath the surface.

McVay snatched Klapper's arms and hauled him onto the raft. Peering into the inky blackness, he could see a few other rafts carrying about fifteen other survivors. Had the sea swallowed the rest of his 1,000-man crew?

JULY 30: *Nagasaki, Japan*

The Home Guard officer, a white-bearded man in his sixties, was training the line of women to use knives, homemade spears, and clubs to kill American invaders.

"If each of you only kill one American," the officer told the women, "you will have done your part to save our home."

One stooped, gray-haired woman was reading a booklet of instructions. She read: "You, a member of a Combat unit for the People's Volunteer Corps, are part of the armed forces of the Imperial fighting services. You, like all Imperial soldiers, must not allow yourself to be taken as prisoner. . . . Nor must you allow yourself to die a dishonorable death."

She watched another woman swinging at a cloth dummy dangling from a rope. "No, no," the instructor scolded the woman. "You must aim at the abdomen. The abdomen."

The woman, a fifty-year-old mother, stared at her weapon. She wondered how she could attack an American soldier's abdomen with a child's hammer.

JULY 31: *In the Pacific Ocean, about 300 miles from Guam*

The tropical sun beat down on men tossing in rafts or bouncing over waves in their life jackets. The salt water licked at bleeding wounds and charred skin.

The *Indianapolis* survivors—about 700 had jumped free of the sinking cruiser—now floated in a widening circle. As far apart as ten miles, men on rafts or swimmers in the water could see only a dozen or so other survivors. They thought they were the only ones alive.

They had tossed in the water for almost thirty-six hours. They had no water, no food.

"Don't drink the water!" sailors shouted to each other.

But some had to wet parched throats. Tongues licked at the salt water. Mouths and throats bloated, and within hours dozens of sailors were dead.

"Hang on, hang on," sailors told each other. They gripped ropes dangling from rafts, which held the badly injured and the dying. The stronger survivors swam in their life jackets from raft to raft, shouting, "Don't give up; we'll be picked up soon! Help will be on the way!"

Only radioman Larry Woods and a few others knew that the Navy thought the *Indianapolis* was still cruising toward the Philippines. No help was on the way.

Chapter Eight

"Sharks! Sharks!"

The sailors shrieked as the grayish fins circled the swimmers. A man screamed, his face twisting in pain. His head bobbed up and down, then vanished. Blood blossomed over where he had gone under.

The *Indianapolis* sailors beat frantically at the water with their hands, trying to scare off the sharks. "Don't stray from the pack!" officers shouted. "Stay close and we can make splashing sounds—they'll keep the sharks away."

The *Indianapolis* survivors now were spread out over thirty miles as they began their third night at sea. Many were thirsty to the point of madness. "The days are bad enough with that hot sun beating down," Ed ("Doc") Haynes, one of the ship's medical officers, was telling another man on a raft. "But the nights are worse because the men see things in the dark that are not there."

That night Haynes heard a swimmer scream, "Here comes a Jap; he's trying to kill me!"

Haynes strained his eyes, scanning the darkness for the pinpoint of a rescue ship's searchlight. Where was his navy when he needed it the most?

AUGUST 1: *Potsdam, Germany*

The meeting of the Big Three was coming to a close with a night of dining and drinking. "Churchill and Stalin, who like staying up late, like these things," Truman wrote in his diary. "But it has been hard for me—an early riser. I want to go home."

The meeting had been "a waste of seventeen working days I could have used at home," he told his new secretary of state, James Byrnes. Stalin had refused to give an inch of the land his armies had taken in Europe. The millions now living under Red Army guns—in Poland, Austria, the Baltic states, Czechoslovakia, Bulgaria, Rumania, Hungary, and East Germany— would be ruled by Moscow.

Truman ended his notes on Potsdam with a warning to himself and the country: "The Russians are planning world conquest."

AUGUST 2: *In the Pacific Ocean, about 300 miles from Guam*

The living stared upward at the bright blue sky. Dead men rolled in the waves, roped by their waists to rafts. They had died during the night. The men still alive were too exhausted to cut the ropes. Their agony had now stretched into its eighty-fourth hour.

A cemetery's stillness hung over the rafts and the swimmers clinging to them. Swollen lips hung open; bearded faces were drawn gaunt; glazed eyes showed the loss of all hope.

A swimmer heard a low drone. He looked up and saw a tiny black speck plastered against the blue sky. Another sailor raised his fist weakly into the air.

"Too high to see us," someone else said. At least two planes had passed over the rafts earlier. They had gone on without seeing the black specks bobbing amid the whitecaps.

But this plane seemed to pause, hanging in the blue. Then it began a slow, lazy turn.

"He sees us! He sees us!" sailors shouted. A few of the stronger ones kicked up a froth with their feet.

Some ten miles away, Captain McVay watched the plane glide down low toward the water. He could see it dropping tiny specks— rafts, he guessed, to swimmers! He now knew there were other survivors besides the thirty or forty men riding on rafts near him.

The plane soared upward and vanished. Hours went by. McVay's eyes were aching as he scanned the horizon. Then he saw another dot that grew larger. It was, McVay realized, a flying boat that could set down on the ocean. He watched it splash down about five miles from his raft. Then came a second flying boat, and he could see—as he rose atop a swell—that it was scooping up swimmers.

Night blacked out his view. But searchlight

beams poked through the blackness. McVay asked the men on nearby rafts to join him in saying the Lord's Prayer.

AUGUST 3: *Aboard a destroyer in the Pacific*

Captain McVay staggered on the deck. Like his fellow survivors, he was covered with sun blisters on his face and arms. He asked how many of his crew had been picked up.

Of the 1,199 men aboard the *Indianapolis,* about 400 went down with the ship. Of the 799 who had endured four days without food or water in a sea of sharks, 316 had survived.

AUGUST 6: *Tinian Island, near Guam*

The stocky, square-shouldered colonel, Paul Tebbets, grinned as he stared at his B-29. Emblazoned on the ship was *Enola Gay,* his mother's name. It was against orders to put real names on bombers. But Tebbets had insisted that this B-29 carry his mother's name as it dropped the first atomic bomb—a mission he knew would make history.

Tebbets watched as the shark-gray bomb, nicknamed Little Boy, was strapped into the B-29's bay. It was about ten feet long and three feet wide, smaller than he had imagined. It weighed 10,000 pounds. Wires ran to fuses plugged into the bomb's skin. The fuses were timed so the bomb would blow up about a quarter of a mile above the target.

At 1:45 A.M., Japanese time, the *Enola Gay*

roared down the runway and rose over the Pacific. Two B-29s trailed behind her. They carried gauges to measure Little Boy's blast.

Tebbets had been told to bomb one of three cities—Nagasaki, Kokura, or Hiroshima. A scout plane, circling over Japan, radioed the *Enola Gay* that clouds hung over the three cities, but Tebbets could drop the bomb through holes in the clouds over Hiroshima. Tebbets swung the nose of the *Enola Gay* toward the seaport city and its 500,000 slumbering residents.

AUGUST 6: *In the* Enola Gay *six miles over Hiroshima, Japan*

The time was exactly 8:00 A.M. "We are about to start the bomb run," Tebbets's voice crackled over the intercom. "Put on your goggles."

The crewmen jerked on goggles that would protect their eyes against the snow-white glare that had lit up the New Mexico desert.

The bombardier stared into his Norden bombsight. He pressed a button. At 8:15 plus seventeen seconds he watched Little Boy tumble from the bomb bay. *Enola Gay* dived to the right, turning rapidly. Tebbets had been told to get away from the target fast.

At 8:16 Little Boy exploded.

Sergeant Robert Caron looked down at what he called "a peep into hell."

A cloud of dust ballooned upward, pushed by a whirling column of white smoke. The cloud spread wide, forming a mushroom-shaped cap some two miles above the *Enola Gay*.

"My God," shouted the copilot, Captain Ben Lewis, "what have we done?"

A minute before, the crew had been looking down at a city shining in the morning sun. Now they were looking into a black pit boiling over with smoke and orange and blue flames.

"Could anyone live through that down there?" someone muttered over the intercom.

Caron suddenly bounced high off his gunner's seat. He saw waves of hot air rippling upward from Hiroshima. As the waves slammed into the B-29, the *Enola Gay* crackled, popped, and groaned. "The *Enola Gay*," remembered Lewis, "was shuddering as if whacked with a telephone pole."

AUGUST 6: *Hiroshima*

The sunny morning had suddenly turned midnight black. "There was no sky left," said Nichiyoshi Nukushina, a fire-truck driver. A small boy wailed to his mother, "Why is it night already?"

They stood at least a dozen miles from the blast center. From a few miles away, five-year-old Sachiko Habu had been watching his mother at prayer in front of the family altar. "My mother," he later said, "was turned into white bones."

The fifty-million-degree heat at the blast

As the poisonous nuclear cloud spread wide to form a mushroom-shaped cap, the copilot of the *Enola Gay* shouted, "My God, what have we done?" *(Photo courtesy of the National Archives)*

center burned roofs a dozen miles away. Telephone poles were charred black. Human beings vanished, leaving only the outlines of their bodies burned into walls and sidewalks.

The heat ignited the air like matches to tissue paper. Curtains of flame stormed through the streets, consuming men and women who had survived the blast's first shock waves. Fierce winds howled in front of the fires. They toppled trees and churned rivers into tidal waves that drowned thousands.

Cries of "Mizu! Mkzu!" ("Water! Water!") rose in the smashed, glass-strewn streets. "The thirst was like a red-hot poker in the throat," said police chief Shiroku Tanube.

Women and men staggered into Hiroshima Communications Hospital with their hair falling out in handfuls. A doctor looked at radiation burns on hands and faces and told another doctor, "We are treating a new sickness."

Out in the street a fourth-grade girl staggered by men and women who were "covered with blood and trailing their torn clothes after them. The skin of their arms was peeled off and dangled from their fingertips, and they walked silently, hanging their arms before them."

A college student saw "screaming children who have lost sight of their mothers, mothers searching for their little ones. Every one among the fleeing was dyed red with blood."

A fifth-grade boy thought, he said, "that all the human beings on the face of the earth had been killed off. And only the five of us, my family, were left behind in an uncanny world of the dead. . . .

"I saw nothing that wasn't burned to a crisp. I saw fire reservoirs filled to the brim with dead people who looked as though they had been boiled alive. In one reservoir there were so many dead people there wasn't enough room for them to fall over. They must have died sitting in the water."

A fifth-grade boy said of this day: "No matter how much I might try to exaggerate, the truth would still be more terrible than even my wildest exaggeration."

AUGUST 6: *Aboard the cruiser* Augusta *in the Atlantic*

President Truman, coming home by sea, was lunching belowdecks with enlisted men. He was joking with sailors from New Jersey and Minnesota when the ship's captain handed him a radio message from Washington.

Truman scanned the first line: "Hiroshima bombed . . . Result Clear Cut Successful."

The President leaped up and shouted, "Captain, this is the greatest thing in history!" He turned to the sailors. His voice rang across the mess hall: "Boys, it's time for us to get home! We have just dropped a new bomb on Japan which has more power than 20,000 tons of TNT."

The sailors stared at one another. What new bomb?

AUGUST 7: *Tokyo, the Office of the Army General Staff*

The Vice Chief of Staff paced impatiently in a room filled with telephone switchboard operators. For the past twenty-four hours, the operators had been trying to place calls to Hiroshima. The last call from Hiroshima had come at about 8:00 A.M. yesterday reporting a lone B-29 crossing the city.

A woman operator suddenly shrieked. The Vice Chief rushed to her side. Her trembling fingers handed him the message she had just scrawled on a piece of paper. The first call from Hiroshima reported that "the whole city of Hiroshima was destroyed instantly by a single bomb."

The Vice Chief hurried toward the office of Foreign Minister Togo.

AUGUST 7: *Tokyo, the Emperor's Imperial Library*

"Genshi bakudan."

Emperor Hirohito nodded knowingly as he heard the words from a general. He knew what a *genshi bakudan,* an atomic bomb, could do. His scientists had tried to build one early in the war. When a scientist blew up himself and two buildings, Japanese atomic research was stopped.

The *genshi bakudan* had killed or injured at least 130,000 people in Hiroshima, the Emperor was told. No air raid had ever inflicted so many casualties.

His cheek twitched nervously as the Emperor spoke in his high-pitched, almost childish voice. He asked if Japan's envoy in Moscow had asked the Russians to appeal to the Americans to start peace talks. He was told that the Russian foreign minister had agreed to speak with the envoy tomorrow.

AUGUST 7: *Washington, the White House*

General Marshall and Secretary Stimson walked into the Oval Office. They looked grim. They told President Truman that Hiroshima was a dead city. But no offer of surrender had come from Tokyo. They said the Air Corps was set to drop a second bomb—this one on Kokura. Truman, his face also grim, gave his approval.

"I don't want to give the signal to start the invasion," Marshall told Truman.

Wait until we see what happens after we drop the bomb on Kokura, Truman told Marshall.

Marshall left the room with a heavy heart. How could he hope that a second bomb—and another 100,000 or so dead or maimed civilians—could do what the first had failed to do?

AUGUST 8: *Tokyo, the Ministry of Foreign Affairs*

Foreign Minister Togo read the message from Ambassador Sato. Sato reported that he had met with Stalin's foreign minister. The Russians had made no offer to talk to the

Americans about peace talks. Instead, Sato was told, Russia was declaring war on Japan immediately.

AUGUST 8: *Tokyo, the Emperor's air-raid bunker under the Imperial Library*

Hirohito and his closest adviser, Lord Privy Seal Koichi, hurried down the concrete steps as sirens wailed in the midnight darkness outside. Servants switched on lights. The Emperor's face glistened with sweat in the humid, smelly underground air. His wife and children slept in a nearby room.

"We should not let slip this opportunity," the Emperor told Koichi. "Now that a weapon of the deadliest power has been used against us," he said, Japan could agree to surrender honorably.

Koichi nodded. Japan's military men, he knew, could surrender and "save face." They would not be humiliated. The world would see that they had surrendered to a weapon no fighting men could defeat.

"Tell Prime Minister Suzuki," the Emperor said, his face twitching violently, "that it is my wish that the war be ended as soon as possible."

AUGUST 9: *Chicago, Illinois*

University of Chicago deans said they expected more than 1,000 ex-GIs to enroll in the fall under the new GI Bill. It gave veterans $1,000 each year to pay for tuition and books, plus up to $75 a month for their living costs. "That guarantees," said a dean, "a free college education for any veteran."

AUGUST 9: *In* Bock's Car, *a B-29 six miles over Kokura, Japan*

The bombardier, Captain Kermit Beahan, stared through the rubber eyepiece of his bombsight. He frowned and shook his head. Fluffy clouds blocked his view of his target, rows of munitions plants.

Bock's Car was carrying the world's second atomic bomb, named Fat Man. It was more powerful, Beahan had been told, than the Fat Man tested last month at Alamogordo.

He couldn't just drop it on a cloud. "No drop!" he shouted on the intercom. He could not see the plants.

Black puffs nipped at the B-29's tail—exploding antiaircraft shells. A waist gunner shouted, "Major, the flak is coming closer."

The pilot, Major Chuck Sweeney, turned *Bock's Car* toward Nagasaki.

AUGUST 9: *In* Bock's Car *over Nagasaki*

Kermit Beahan's eyes strained to find the target, ground zero, which sat in the middle of the Mitsubishi war plants. But he could see only thickening clouds.

Beads of sweat were forming on the forehead of Major Sweeney in the pilot's seat. His plane was running out of gas. He had to drop the bomb on this run or drop the world's most expensive weapon in the ocean. He could not hang over Japan a minute longer.

A voice—Beahan's—suddenly filled Sweeney's earphones. A hole had popped open in a cloud, Beahan said. He could see a valley a mile or so from ground zero.

"I'll take it," Beahan told Sweeney. He pressed a button.

Bock's Car lifted violently into the air, suddenly lighter by five tons. Fat Man swayed in its parachute as it dropped to a mile above Nagasaki. The crew saw a bluish white flame. There was a roar that blasted through their earphones.

"Well, Bea," a gunner said to the bombardier, "there's 100,000 Japs you just killed."

AUGUST 9: *Nagasaki*

Dr. Tatsuichiro Akizuki heard the plane roar about the roof of Urakami Hospital as he stood over a patient's bed. "It's an enemy plane," he shouted. "Look out—take cover!"

He dropped to the floor. "There was a blinding white flash of light," he remembered. "A huge impact like a gigantic blow smote down on our bodies, our heads, and our hospital. I lay flat . . . then down came piles of debris."

He staggered to his feet, hearing pleas: "Help me, doctor!" As he crawled through the debris toward patients strewn across the room, Dr. Akizuki looked toward the valley.

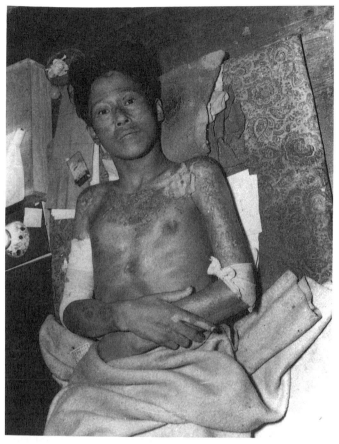

A victim of the bombing of Nagasaki. Actually, more people died or were injured during the firebombings of Japan early in 1945 than were killed or injured during the atomic bombings of Hiroshima and Nagasaki. *(Photo courtesy of the National Archives)*

"All the buildings I could see were on fire. . . . Trees on the nearby hills were smoking. . . . It seemed as if the earth itself emitted fire. . . . It seemed like the end of the world."

He took some of the badly burned to a nearby river.

"Half-naked or nearly naked people were

crouching at the water's edge. . . . On one side their bodies had been grilled and were highly inflamed."

These "white ghosts," as he called them, "were working in the fields when the bomb fell. The moment they turned to look up, their faces as well as their backs were burnt by the flash. It seemed to me like a picture of hell, seeing those groaning half-naked people."

AUGUST 10: *Tokyo, the Emperor's bunker under the Imperial Library*

The Big Six, as they were called, avoided each other's eyes. The Emperor's haggard appearance made them feel embarrassed. The Japanese people looked up to Hirohito as a direct descendant of God. But now, his shoulders twitching, he seemed all too human.

Hirohito seldom met with the Big Six—two military men and four cabinet ministers. He had allowed them to make the nation's big decisions as they steered Japan through almost ten years of war.

By now, 2:30 A.M., Hirohito and the Big Six knew that more than 70,000 had died in Nagasaki. At least another 290,000 in Nagasaki and Hiroshima were injured or homeless. Hundreds were dying daily, many in agony, their bodies poisoned by the deadly radiation still in the air above the two flattened cities.

Three of the Big Six wanted Japan to fight on. Three wanted to ask for terms of surrender.

Premier Suzuki rose. A decision must be made—and soon, he said.

He turned to face the throne. "His Majesty's wish," he said, "must settle the issue."

A general gasped. No one had ever thrown a challenge so directly into the face of the god-like emperor.

There was a long silence. Then Hirohito began to speak: "I cannot bear to have my innocent people suffer further. . . . I have decided to bring the war to an end. That is why I agree to the Foreign Minister's proposal."

Foreign Minister Togo had proposed that Japan surrender with one condition—"the Emperor must remain as Japan's ruler."

Hirohito stood up and left the room. The Big Six sat quietly, staring into space. Several bowed their heads and wept.

Togo quickly sent cables to Japan's ambassadors in neutral Sweden and Switzerland. He ordered the ambassadors to hand messages to the American ambassadors in those countries. Japan would surrender.

AUGUST 10: *Washington, the White House, the Oval Office*

President Truman listened with his top military advisers as Secretary of State James Byrnes read the cables that had just come in from Sweden and Switzerland. The Japanese would surrender—but not unconditionally. Japan's condition: It must keep its Emperor.

Byrnes argued that America should insist on unconditional surrender. Secretary of the Navy James Forrestal disagreed. He told Truman that America should say yes, we accept the offer. But America, he said, should add a big "if": The Emperor could stay only if the Japanese people decided in a free election that he should stay.

Truman told Byrnes to send this message to the Japanese: The Emperor could keep his throne—but only by "the freely expressed will of the people."

A general told Truman that General LeMay could drop another Fat Man on Japan within the week.

Truman thought for a few minutes, then said, "Stop the atom bombing. The thought of wiping out another hundred thousand people is too horrible. I don't like the idea of killing all those kids."

AUGUST 12: *Tokyo, the Imperial Palace*

Lord Privy Seal Marquis Kido bowed in front of the throne. He told Hirohito that the American reply to the Japanese offer to surrender had just been received. The Americans were demanding, he told the Emperor, that the people of Japan be allowed to vote freely on the future of their Emperor.

Hirohito's voice was firm. "If the people don't want an emperor," he told Kido, "all will be futile. I think I can trust the people."

AUGUST 14: *Washington, the White House, the Oval Office*

T ruman stared glumly out the window. He had stayed at his desk all day yesterday, Sunday, and today, Monday, waiting for word that Japan had agreed to surrender. Now it was late in the afternoon, well past three o'clock. He feared that if two atomic blasts would not bring Japan to its knees, he would have to go ahead with the invasion—the cost, another million dead and wounded American fighting men.

The phone rang. Calling was Secretary of State Byrnes. A Swiss diplomat was speeding in a limousine toward the White House with a message from Tokyo. The Japanese had agreed to surrender.

Two hours later Truman fidgeted nervously with his steel-rimmed spectacles as he faced a mob of reporters. He spoke into radio and movie newsreel microphones.

"I have received this afternoon a message from the Japanese government. . . . I deem this reply a full recognition of the Potsdam Declaration, which specified the unconditional surrender of Japan."

Rumors that the war had finally ended for the United States—after three years, eight months, and five days—had brought crowds that jammed Pennsylvania Avenue in front of the White House. They roared as Truman came out onto a balcony and told them: "This is a great day, a day we have all been looking to see for so long. It is a great day for democracy for we have finally defeated . . . the police state."

Truman ordered a two-day national holiday. "Tomorrow, Wednesday, August 15," he said, "will be the official V-J Day. But let's also take another day off on Thursday, August 16, to celebrate. No school for the kids, no work for everybody."

AUGUST 14: *Chicago, Illinois*

Mrs. Frances Evans Dyke heard the news of the surrender on her radio. She was the mother of eleven men who had joined the Army, Navy, and Marines. Four were training to invade Japan. She had much to be thankful for. All eleven of her sons were coming home.

AUGUST 14: *Seattle, Washington*

The sailor was strolling with his wife on Pike Street when a neighbor dashed out of his house. The neighbor was shouting that the Japanese had surrendered.

"What are your plans?" the sailor was asked.

"Have babies and never leave home!" he said, kissing his wife.

Nearby, at Victory Square, Mrs. Viola Ruth Lander sat on a bench, sobbing quietly. She told a soldier that her son, Ted, nineteen, had been killed on Okinawa in May.

"For mothers like me," she told the soldier, "the war will never really be over."

AUGUST 14: *San Francisco, California*

The trolley car raced down the long, steep hill. A grinning sailor stood at the controls. The car was packed with sailors, soldiers, and girls, all singing loudly, "God Bless America."

AUGUST 14: *Salt Lake City, Utah*

The rain streamed down on the soldiers and civilians snake-dancing through the dark street. They were doing the popular Conga dance, shouting, "One, two, three . . . and KICK!"

"Getting soaked," said one sailor, kissing a girl, "and loving it."

AUGUST 14: *St. Louis, Missouri*

The crowd surged through the streets near the Mississippi bridges, blowing whistles and banging pots and pans. The crowd turned a corner and faced the gates of a church. A clergyman was opening the gates. The crowd filed into the church, and the clergyman began to say prayers of thanksgiving.

AUGUST 19: *Manila*

The half-dozen Japanese delegates sat stiffly in their chairs, facing MacArthur's chief of staff, General Dick Sutherland. He was giving them General MacArthur's orders on how the Japanese should surrender.

American troops, Sutherland said, would

land at Atsugi airport near Yokahama on August 23. Some five days later, he said, General MacArthur would land at Atsugi. And on September 2, on the battleship *Missouri,* anchored in Tokyo Bay, the Japanese delegates would sign the formal papers of surrender.

At the word *Atsugi,* the Japanese delegates stared at one another.

Don't land at Atsugi, one delegate told Sutherland. The Japanese could not guarantee the safety of any American, especially MacArthur, who landed at Atsugi. The airport was a hotbed of kamikaze pilots. They had sworn blood oaths to kill Americans rather than surrender.

Sutherland told MacArthur of the danger. But MacArthur only shrugged. His troops would land at Atsugi, he said, and so would he.

AUGUST 19: *Near Mukden, Manchuria*

Paratrooper Major Bob Lamar walked through the gates of the camp where the Japanese were holding American prisoners of war. The Japanese guards glared at Lamar, but officers had ordered them not to stop the freeing of the prisoners.

Lamar was one of hundreds of paratroopers being air-dropped across China and Manchuria. Their mission: to free quickly all American prisoners and get them to hospitals.

Lamar stared at the hollow-eyed faces and bony bodies of the Americans who shuffled toward him, too weak to show their happiness. Lamar told a Japanese guard to bring General Jonathan Wainwright to him immediately.

After General MacArthur had escaped from the Philippines to Australia early in 1942, Wainwright had taken command of the 75,000-man American-Filipino army. Within a few weeks he was forced to surrender his starving and sick soldiers to the Japanese, a surrender that was the worst defeat in U.S. military history.

Wainwright shuffled into a room where Lamar and a Japanese officer waited. The tall, thin Wainwright had endured more than 1,000 days of starvation, beatings, and humiliations. He stood stiffly at attention.

"Sit down, General," Lamar said, offering him a chair.

"No!" snapped the officer. "The prisoner will stand."

"General Wainwright will sit," Lamar shot back.

But Wainwright still stood at attention. "Are you really an American?" he whispered fearfully to Lamar.

Wainwright had heard no news in months. He did not know that the war was over. Lamar told him of the surrender.

Wainwright had worried for three years that Americans back home were accusing him of being a traitor. He asked Lamar if he would be tried at a court-martial for having surrendered on Bataan.

"General, you're a hero back home."
Wainwright still stood at attention. He could not believe he was a free man, or that he was a hero back home.

AUGUST 26: *Utsunomiya, Japan*

Women workers at the Nakajima Aircraft Company requested that they be given poison pills so they could die quickly before they were assaulted by the occupying Americans.

AUGUST 27: *Mukden, Manchuria*

Hours earlier General Wainwright had arrived here by train with other former prisoners. Air Corps C-47 transports stood on runways, waiting to fly the thin, bent men to hospitals in Manila. Wainwright walked toward a C-47, leaning heavily on a cane.

An American major came up to Wainwright, saluted, and said, "Sir, we have a message from General MacArthur. He requests that you join him on the deck of the battleship *Missouri* for the surrender by the Japanese."

Wainwright turned and began to walk toward a plane that would take him to the surrender in Tokyo Bay. He was walking, the major noticed, without the help of the cane.

AUGUST 28: *Atsugi airport outside Yokahama, Japan*

General MacArthur's personal B-17, the *Bataan*, rolled down the runway, spun on its wheels, and coughed to a stop. MacArthur

stepped out the door. He saw General Bob Eichelberger waiting to greet him. "Fighting
Bob" Eichelberger had led MacArthur's troops
in turning back the Japanese tide sweeping
toward Australia in the dark days of 1942.

"Bob," said MacArthur, "from Melbourne
to Tokyo is a long way. But this seems to be the
end of the road."

Eichelberger stared uneasily around the airfield. One bullet from the hidden rifle of a kamikaze could mean the end of the road for his
chief.

No one would shoot at him, MacArthur
told Eichelberger. They climbed into a battered
limousine. The car bucked and backfired as it
swayed toward Yokahama some twenty miles
away. At each explosion, MacArthur's officers
snatched for their pistols.

"Look!" an officer shouted as the car swung
onto a road into the city.

Rifle-carrying Japanese troops lined each
side of the road. The soldiers stood with their
backs to the passing car.

They stood ready to protect him, MacArthur told his officers, because he had come as
their conqueror. Their turned backs, he said,
were "a sign of respect—the same token of respect they would show for the authority of their
Emperor."

AUGUST 31: *Yokahama*

MacArthur was eating dinner in a hotel.
Tomorrow he would leave for the surren-

A haggard General Jonathan Wainwright is welcomed to freedom by his old chief, General MacArthur. Wainwright endured over three years of beatings and starvation in Japanese prison camps. Expecting a traitor's homecoming, Wainwright was hailed a hero. *(Photo courtesy of the National Archives)*

der ceremony on September 2 in Tokyo Bay aboard the *Missouri*.

An officer hurried into the dining room. He told MacArthur that General Wainwright had just arrived. MacArthur rose quickly and rushed to the lobby. He saw the man he had left in a cave to fight the hopeless battle for Bataan.

Wainwright stood stiffly as his old chief came toward him. Wainwright's newly starched, suntan uniform hung stiffly on his straw-thin shoulders. MacArthur embraced him, repeating his nickname, "Jim . . . Jim . . ." in a choked voice.

MacArthur led Wainwright to his table. Wainwright told MacArthur how he had feared he would be tried as a traitor for having surrendered on Bataan.

"Jim," MacArthur said, "when you go home, the President is waiting to pin on you the Congressional Medal of Honor."

Chapter Nine

SEPT. 2: *On the deck of the* Missouri *in Tokyo Bay*

The band played "The Star-Spangled Banner" as the eleven members of the Japanese surrender delegation stood rigidly at attention. They gripped their black silk top hats to keep the breeze from blowing them away. They wore formal morning suits with coattails, high collars, and white gloves. They looked straight ahead, many with moist eyes. They avoided the stares of gum-chewing American sailors perched on the *Missouri*'s gun barrels and clustered on her gun turrets.

The masts of hundreds of American and allied warships rose high into the sky above Tokyo Bay. Their crews grouped near radios to hear the broadcast of the surrender. The broadcast would be recorded and heard in America and Europe, where the date was September 1, 1945. World War II was ending six years to the day after its beginning with the German invasion of Poland.

MacArthur strode onto the deck of the *Missouri*. He stood at a table covered with a green cloth, facing the Japanese. At his side were the

Crewmen of the battleship *Missouri* cram every inch of the decks for the best possible viewing spot of the surrender ceremonies. The Japanese delegates arrived in top hats and formal attire. It was no accident that the *Missouri* was picked as the surrender site; Missouri was Truman's home state. *(Photo courtesy of the National Archives)*

commanders who had brought Japan to this table: Wainwright, Halsey, Nimitz, Kenney, and Eichelberger among them.

His hands shaking with emotion, MacArthur read from a sheet of paper: "The terms and conditions upon which the surrender of the Japanese Imperial Forces is here to be given and accepted . . ."

One by one the Japanese delegates stepped forward, took off their gloves and top hats, and signed surrender documents. MacArthur signed for the United States. He was followed

General MacArthur signs the surrender papers. Standing behind him are Generals Wainwright and Arthur Percivel, whose armies were defeated by the Japanese in Malaya earlier in the war. (Photo courtesy of the National Archives)

by generals and admirals of more than a dozen members of the United Nations.

A roaring filled the sky above the *Missouri*. From the far horizon came wave after wave of American and Allied warplanes. More than 2,000 planes zoomed by in a final flyover salute to the men and women, alive and dead, who had won World War II.

As the thunder died away over the distant Mount Fuji, MacArthur delivered a last message to the people of America, listening back home: "Today, the guns are silent," he said. "A great tragedy has ended. A great victory has been won. The skies no longer rain death. The seas bear only commerce. Men everywhere walk upright in the sunlight. The entire world is quietly at peace."

POSTSCRIPT

Humankind would not live long in peace after the end of World War II. In July 1946, Winston Churchill dragged into the open the growing distrust between Communist Soviet Russia and the Western democracies. In a speech at Fulton, Missouri, he charged that Stalin had dropped an "Iron Curtain" between eastern and western Europe.

The cold war that followed did not erupt into World War III, as many had feared. Nuclear warheads remained underground, and the world was spared a meltdown that certainly would have resulted in more deaths than the more than twenty million dead in World War II.

The tide of the war was turned when the United States entered the battle in 1941. It was won by the courage of American fighting men and women and by the know-how never before seen in modern industrial engineering. America built a military colossus of ships, tanks, planes, and guns that armed the entire world.

Some historians have called World War II "the last good war." It was good for Americans to stop Japan and Germany from enslaving half

A last salute to those who didn't come home. *(Photo courtesy of the National Archives)*

the world. No war, however, cost so much in lost lives, maimed and crippled bodies, ruined cities, families torn apart, and the horrors of the Holocaust. Time after time, outnumbered Americans defeated the enemy at places never to be forgotten, notably Midway and Bastogne.

It is fifty years after the surrender on the battleship *Missouri*. Today's Americans can look back on the years from Pearl Harbor in 1941 to Tokyo Bay in 1945 and say with pride and gratitude to their parents and grandparents who fought its battles, "Well done!"

CHIANG

CHURCHILL

DE GAULLE

EISENHOWER

HIROHITO

HITLER

MACARTHUR

MARSHALL

ROMMEL

ROOSEVELT

STALIN

TOJO

TRUMAN

CHIANG
KAI-SHEK
1887–1975

The son of peasants, Chiang Kai-shek (spelled Jiang Jieshi in Chinese) teamed with warlords to form a Nationalist army in the 1920s that overthrew the government. He feuded with the Communist leader, Mao Tse-tung (Zedong in Chinese), ousted the Communists from his Nationalist Party, and set up a government in Peking (now Beijing). In 1937 the Japanese invaded China and cleared Mao's and Chiang's armies from cities along the coast. Chiang and Mao hid out in mountains.

Roosevelt sent weapons to China, even though his CBI (China-Burma-India Theater) commander, General Joe ("Vinegar Joe") Stilwell, told him that Chiang and his generals were corrupt and that his seven-million-man army was poorly trained and led. Stilwell saw that Chiang was more interested in keeping himself in power with American weapons in his hands than in risking his troops against the Japanese.

Roosevelt and Stilwell tried to cajole Chiang into re-taking nearby Burma. Chiang cooperated only when assured that the British would join in the attack. Shortly after World War II, Mao's Communist armies overthrew Chiang, forcing him to retreat to the island of Formosa. There, guarded by U.S. warships, he set up a Nationalist China that has survived, at times uneasily, side by side with Communist China.

WINSTON CHURCHILL
1874–1965

Winston Spencer Churchill caught the eyes of Britishers at the turn of the century as a dashing soldier, journalist, and author. During World War I he led the British navy as its first lord of the admiralty. In 1940 he became prime minister, his ringing speeches steeling the British will to win despite their early defeats in World War II.

He prayed for America to join the war against Hitler. Right after the attack on Pearl Harbor, he sped to Washington to convince Roosevelt that Hitler should be defeated first, then Japan.

Churchill considered himself a master military strategist and told British generals what to do. The American General Marshall often disagreed with his ideas on winning the war, but Churchill usually got his way by charming Roosevelt.

Churchill balked at an invasion of France in 1942 and again in 1943. He favored a drive through Italy or Yugoslavia. But Stalin let it be known that he might sign a peace treaty with Hitler if there was no invasion of France in 1944.

In 1944 and 1945 Churchill tried to make deals with Stalin concerning which postwar European countries would be pro-West and which pro-East. But Stalin set up Communist puppet governments in East Berlin and all across eastern Europe. Churchill, voted out of power in 1945, watched helplessly. In 1946 he said Stalin had dropped an "Iron Curtain" across Europe. That began the cold war. In the 1950s, again prime minister, Churchill tried to "contain" the spread of communism around the globe while watching colonies like India become independent, his beloved British Empire breaking up.

Charles

de Gaulle
1890-1970

A graduate of St. Cyr, France's West Point, de Gaulle was wounded during World War I and later taken prisoner by the Germans. During the 1920s and 1930s he became the French army's expert on tank warfare. But French generals believed that tanks could be stopped by their concrete Maginot Line stretching between France and Germany.

After Hitler's panzers swept around the Maginot Line in 1940 and France collapsed, de Gaulle went to England. He formed a Free French army that fought side by side with the British in Syria and Egypt against the Italians and Germans.

Roosevelt distrusted and disliked the haughty de Gaulle, who boasted "I am France!" But de Gaulle elbowed aside other French generals to become the leader of the Free French government-in-exile. And in 1944, as the Allies liberated France, Churchill supported de Gaulle in his efforts to become the leader of postwar France. Churchill feared that France might be ruled after the war by Communists, whom de Gaulle was trying to keep out of the French government.

By 1945 Roosevelt had overcome his personal dislike for de Gaulle. He knew that de Gaulle had become a symbol of a "free France" to the people of liberated French cities. De Gaulle marched into those cities leading his Free French soldiers. He pushed aside pro-Communists and other politicians. After the war he and his de Gaullists would govern postwar France for much of twenty years.

DWIGHT D. EISENHOWER
1890–1969

Born in Texas, Eisenhower grew up in Abilene, Kansas. He graduated from West Point in 1915 but did not command troops in World War I. From 1935 to 1939 he helped set up the American-Filipino army under General MacArthur. In 1941 Marshall made him chief of war planning. He was sent to England to command a cross-Channel invasion of France. But when Churchill and Roosevelt decided instead on invading North Africa, Marshall selected Eisenhower as commander.

A worrier in private, Eisenhower flashed a sunny smile in public that said all was going well. General Patton thought he gave British generals, like Bernard Montgomery, everything they wanted. But Ike, as he was called, believed that getting along with the British was a necessity for victory.

In 1944 Eisenhower took command of the largest invasion force in history. His troops landed in France after a stormy crossing, smashed through France, and by late 1944 seemed to have defeated Germany. But a German attack surprised him, costing heavy casualties. In 1945 he decided not to try to beat the Soviets to Berlin, a decision that angered Churchill. After the war Eisenhower won the presidency twice, in 1952 and 1956. During his second term he refused French pleas to involve the United States in the Vietnam War.

EMPEROR

HIROHITO

1901–1989

In the presence of an emperor they looked up to as a god, even crusty Japanese generals like Hideki Tojo felt their knees wobble when a faint look of displeasure crossed Hirohito's face.

Hirohito ascended to his father's throne in 1926. In 1931 the Japanese began to expand the Empire of the Rising Sun by conquering China's Manchuria. In 1937 they attacked China to acquire more land and natural resources. The Emperor did not forbid these land grabs by the military. Like the military, he believed the growing population of Japan could survive only by acquiring land, rice, and oil.

A quiet-spoken man who liked poetry, he questioned pilots after the attack on Pearl Harbor and wanted to be assured that no hospitals or schools had been attacked. Believing that American airmen had shot at children during the Doolittle raid in 1942 (they had not), he approved the executions of three of the captured flyers.

By 1944 Hirohito realized that Japan had lost the war. When his brother suggested that Japan seek peace, he balked, fearful that the Americans would depose an emperor his people revered as divine. But when Truman signaled that Hirohito could remain as emperor with the people's approval, he agreed to the surrender. He quickly forged a strong, friendly partnership with General MacArthur, Japan's military governor, as Japan became a democracy and an industrial power.

Adolf Hitler
1889–1945

Hitler was born in Linz, Austria. As a teenager he went to Vienna to attend an art academy, but was rejected. Humiliated, he became a homeless person. As a World War I corporal, he survived four years of bloody trench war. He blamed Germany's defeat on Jews and Communists, claiming they "stabbed Germany in the back." As leader of the popular Nazi Party, he became Germany's chancellor in 1933 and built up the German army. Europe's war-weary leaders watched as he grabbed land, including his native Austria. World War II broke out when he attacked Poland in 1939.

Hitler's fast-moving troops and tanks conquered western Europe, besieged England, and swept to the gates of Moscow until the Red Army drove him back. Up to that point his generals had thought he was a military genius. But bloody defeats in Soviet Russia, Africa, Italy, and France in 1943 and 1944 made them realize they were being led by a madman. They tried to assassinate him several times, but each plot failed.

By 1944 Hitler had become a twitching physical wreck, his body damaged by disease and drugs. His generals followed his often-hysterical orders, knowing his SS troops would torture and kill them if they disobeyed. He hid in an underground bunker in Berlin as Soviet and German troops battled inside the city. If captured alive, he said, the Soviets would parade him in a cage through the streets of Moscow. As Berlin burned above his bunker, Hitler married a longtime companion, Eva Braun, and together they committed suicide.

DOUGLAS MACARTHUR
1880–1964

Macarthur's father, General Arthur MacArthur, had won the Congressional Medal of Honor in the Civil War. His son, Douglas, graduated from West Point in 1903 and led troops in frontline battles in France during World War I. By the 1930s he was Army chief of staff and fought bitterly with President Roosevelt over more money for defense. He retired and became a military adviser to the Filipino army. In 1941 Roosevelt made him commander of the American-Filipino army.

In mid-December of 1941, Japan's veteran troops invaded the Philippines and routed MacArthur's army. But he surprised the Japanese by slipping his troops into the jungle peninsula of Bataan. His soldiers held Bataan for more than three months, disease and hunger finally forcing them to surrender. MacArthur escaped to Australia promising, "I shall return!" He had become America's number one war hero. Some Republicans wanted him as their candidate for president in 1944.

MacArthur adopted as his own an idea of Washington strategists—"island hopping" around Japanese strongholds. In 1943 and 1944 he used the strategy brilliantly as his forces leaped thousands of miles, landing in the Philippines by late 1944. MacArthur could boast (and he did) that his men suffered fewer casualties than the forces of any other World War II commander. In 1945 Roosevelt named him supreme commander of the forces invading Japan. He arranged the Japanese surrender and then became the military ruler of occupied Japan. Idolized by the people he had conquered, MacArthur showed that war-torn nation how to become an industrial power and a democracy.

GEORGE C. MARSHALL
1880–1959

The son of a Pennsylvania coal executive, George Catlett Marshall attended Virginia Military Institute. During World War I in France, he rose to become a colonel on the staff of the commander of the American Expeditionary Force. He and another young AEF officer, Douglas MacArthur, had run-ins. As chief of staff in the 1930s, MacArthur slowed Marshall's rise in the military hierarchy. But in 1939 Roosevelt asked Marshall to become chief of staff.

During the first two years of the war, Marshall growled angrily as Roosevelt approved ideas proposed by Churchill—such as the invasion of North Africa— that Marshall opposed. But by 1943, Roosevelt relied heavily on Marshall. He asked him to stay as chief of staff while giving to Eisenhower the prize that Marshall had been promised—commanding the 1944 invasion of France.

Marshall was often called "a soldier's soldier." He was respected for his blunt honesty. In 1947 President Truman made him his secretary of state. He began a plan to rebuild war-shattered Europe. His "Marshall Plan," as it was called, poured $13 billion of American money into Europe, building the industrial democracies of France, Germany, Italy, and other nations. In 1953 he was awarded the Nobel Peace Prize.

ERWIN ROMMEL
1891–1944

The son of an impoverished schoolteacher, Erwin Rommel grew up in an army where most generals were wealthy Prussian noblemen. Machines fascinated him, and he became expert on the strategic use of tanks and armored cars—commanding what the Germans would make famous as Panzer (armored) troops. He argued with older officers that modern battles would be won by armies hitting with speed and surprise.

The stocky, blue-eyed Rommel caught Hitler's attention in 1940 during the conquest of France. Leading his tanks and armored cars at the front, Rommel used speed and daring to surprise and trap millions of Allied soldiers. In 1941 Hitler sent him to North Africa to organize the Afrika Korps. Rommel's tanks drove through Egypt but ran out of gas at the Battle of El Alamein, and he had to retreat to Tunisia. He battled an invading English-American army and was overwhelmed, escaping as 250,000 of his troops surrendered.

Hitler asked Rommel to take over his West Wall on the coast of France and repel the 1944 invasion. Rommel was wounded severely by a strafing Spitfire. Hitler suspected—wrongly—that Rommel had plotted to kill him. He was given the choice of a public trial or committing suicide. Fearing his wife and children would be killed, Rommel chose suicide.

FRANKLIN
DELANO
ROOSEVELT
1882–1945

The son of a wealthy New York State merchant, Roosevelt was graduated from Harvard and became a New York City lawyer. He served in World War I as assistant secretary of the Navy and ran for vice president in 1920. He and his running mate, James Cox, lost. Soon after, he was stricken by infantile paralysis and was bound to a wheelchair the rest of his life.

Charming in person and an eloquent speaker, Roosevelt was elected governor of New York in 1928. And in 1932, he was elected president. He steered the country out of the Great Depression. He despised dictators and sought ways, not always legal, to help the British defeat Hitler.

Roosevelt's big grin and reassuring voice heartened Americans during defeats in 1941 and 1942. He refereed arguments between Churchill and American strategists, making final decisions that usually, but not always, favored British thinking.

By 1944 his aides knew that Roosevelt was a sick man. He was reelected in November and went to Yalta early in 1945 to confer with Stalin and Churchill. To Churchill's dismay, Roosevelt seemed to lack the strength to argue with Stalin over the spread of communism in postwar Europe. During the last six months of the war, Roosevelt handed over most of the details of war strategy to General Marshall. He foresaw the postwar breakup of the British empire and the rise of independent nations in Africa and Asia. He had high hopes for the postwar peacemaking success of the organization that he had named the United Nations.

JOSEF STALIN
1879–1953

Studying to be an Orthodox priest when he was fifteen, Josef Stalin instead became a revolutionary. After the Bolsheviks overthrew the Czar during World War I, Stalin became the right-hand man of the Communist leader, Nikolai Lenin. People in Moscow said, "Lenin trusts Stalin, but Stalin trusts no one." After the death of Lenin, Stalin killed or deported rivals and became a cruel and feared dictator.

In 1939 Stalin shocked the world by signing a non-aggression pact with Hitler, who had sworn to destroy communism. When Hitler double-crossed him by attacking Soviet Russia in 1941, Stalin asked for guns and planes from England and America. He gathered brilliant strategists around him, notably Georgi Zhukov, while his factories turned out tanks and planes at a rate that astonished Hitler.

In 1942 and 1943, Stalin demanded a second front in France that would sandwich Hitler between his armies and the American-British armies. He suspected that England and America wanted to let Hitler's Fascists and his Communists grind each other into dust.

By 1944 Stalin's Red Army had shoved Hitler's armies out of Soviet Russia. The Soviets crunched through Bulgaria, Rumania, Hungary, Austria, and Poland to the German border. Violating promises made at Yalta, Stalin set up "satellite" pro-Communist regimes in the nations his troops had conquered. He feared the United States, Britain, and the capitalist West would gang up to destroy him and communism after the war was won. In 1946 Churchill charged that Stalin had dropped an "Iron Curtain" over eastern Europe, the first shot in what would become the "cold war."

HIDEKI TOJO

1884–1948

Tojo was one of the Japanese military leaders who believed that the island nation of Japan had to expand into the Asian mainland in order to prosper. He became Japan's war minister in the early 1930s. In 1941 Japan's military men chose him to be prime minister.

During the triumphs of 1942, Tojo boasted that Japan would make Asia prosperous for Asians by driving out the Dutch, English, and French colonists. He became jealous of the successes of General Tomoyuki Yamashita in conquering Malaya and the Philippines, and kept him from a major command. At the same time he believed the boasts of his generals and admirals that they could repel attacks by the Americans. He failed to recognize that the navy and army commanders often exaggerated their strength in reports to Tokyo. They feared they would be labeled defeatists if they told the truth—that they were usually outgunned and outnumbered by the Americans and Australians.

By 1944 Emperor Hirohito had become angry as the promised "certain victories" turned into bloody defeats. In July he requested Tojo's resignation as prime minister. After the war Tojo was tried as a war ciminal and executed.

HARRY S TRUMAN
1884–1972

Harry Truman grew up on a farm near Lamar, Missouri. During World War I he yearned to go to France but was rejected by the regular Army because of poor eyesight. He joined the National Guard and went overseas as a major, serving in a field artillery unit.

When the war ended, Truman came back to a depression-ridden country and opened a men's clothing store in Kansas City that failed. Under the guidance of a powerful political boss, he was elected to a judgeship in 1936 and later to the U.S. Senate.

During the war years, Truman headed a Senate investigative committee that looked into the building of war materials by civilian contractors. He found a number of scandals. One of the most shocking was an airplane manufacturer whose slipshod work resulted in the wings falling off its airplanes when in combat.

In 1944, Roosevelt switched his vice presidential candidate from Henry Wallace to Harry Truman, much to Truman's surprise. Roosevelt's sudden death changed Truman abruptly from a humble man to a determined man. He said he never lost one hour of sleep in deciding to drop the atom bomb on Japan.

After the war, Truman poured billions of dollars into Europe as part of what was called the Marshall Plan. He shared Churchill's fear that the Soviet Union was determined to spread communism around the globe. When communist North Korea invaded South Korea in 1950, Truman ordered United Nations forces to go into action and stop the invasion.

Truman became famous for the quote "The buck stops here." When tough decisions had to be made, Truman made them.

IMPORTANT DATES

JANUARY

Jan. 9 General MacArthur's army lands on Luzon, the main island of the Philippines, and advances toward Manila. **Jan. 12** At the request of General Eisenhower and Churchill, Stalin begins a massive attack in the east to draw German troops away from the west, giving Eisenhower's Battle of the Bulge fighters a rest. **Jan. 17** As the Soviet attack shatters Hitler's eastern wall, the Red Army takes Warsaw. **Jan. 21** Hungary quits the war, signing an armistice with the Soviets, Americans, and British. **Jan. 21** A British-Indian force begins an offensive to retake Burma.

FEBRUARY

Feb. 4–11 Roosevelt, Churchill, and Stalin meet at Yalta in the Russian Crimea. They argue over postwar borders of Europe and the carving up of Germany. Stalin makes vague promises of free elections for the people of eastern Europe. **Feb. 5** Japanese sailors begin a defense of Manila, savagely killing civilians. **Feb. 13** The Red Army takes Budapest. **Feb. 19** Marines land on the island of Iwo Jima. **Feb. 23** The American flag is hoisted atop Iwo Jima's Mount Suribachi. **Feb. 26** MacArthur's paratroopers retake the fortress of Corregidor in Luzon's Manila Bay.

MARCH

March 3 Manila is taken by MacArthur's army after 20,000 Japanese defenders are killed along with at least 50,000 civilians. **March 7** Eisenhower's troops cross the Rhine,

Germany's natural defense barrier, at Remagen when the
Germans fail to blow up a bridge. **March 9–10** American
Super Fortresses firebomb Tokyo, killing at least 100,000 civilians. **March 26** Marines wipe out the last Iwo Jima defenders. **March 28** Eisenhower sends a cable to Stalin
saying he intends to bypass Berlin and aim for southern Germany. Churchill protests to Roosevelt that Eisenhower should
try to take Berlin for political reasons, but Eisenhower's decision is upheld by General Marshall.

APRIL

April 1 American soldiers and marines land on Okinawa,
only about 350 miles from Japan. **April 2** Two U.S. armies
link up to trap more than 250,000 Germans near the Rhine.
April 12 President Roosevelt dies suddenly, felled by a
stroke. Harry S Truman becomes president. **April 13**
The death camps of Belsen and Buchenwald are liberated by
American forces. **April 21** Soviet tanks enter a suburb of
Berlin. **April 21** American, Polish, Canadian, and British
Fifth Army troops take Bologna as German resistance in
northern Italy begins to collapse. **April 25** Delegates to
the United Nations conference in San Francisco begin to
draw up a charter for a new postwar peacekeeping organization. **April 28** Former Italian dictator Benito Mussolini
is executed by Italian partisans. **April 30** Adolf Hitler
commits suicide in an underground bunker in Berlin with Soviet troops less than a mile away.

MAY

May 2 Berlin is taken by the Red Army. **May 2** German
forces in Italy surrender as the American Fifth Army pushes
toward the southern gateway to Germany. **May 2** The
British take Rangoon, completing their conquest of Burma.
May 7 German officers sign an unconditional surrender at
Eisenhower's headquarters, agreeing to end the war in Europe near midnight on May 8.

JUNE

June 22   The fighting on Okinawa ends after the deaths of more than 140,000 Japanese soldiers and civilians. Almost 13,000 American soldiers, sailors, and marines are killed, 35,000 wounded. More than 400 navy ships are sunk or damaged by kamikaze attacks.   **June 26**   Delegates from 50 countries sign the United Nations charter.

JULY

July 5   MacArthur's forces complete the liberation of the Philippines.   **July 16**   The world's first atomic bomb is tested successfully in New Mexico.   **July 17–Aug. 2**   Truman, Stalin, and Churchill meet in Potsdam, near Berlin, to discuss postwar Europe. Churchill is replaced midway through the talks by his successor, Clement Attlee. Truman issues what is called the Potsdam Declaration, demanding Japan's unconditional surrender and hinting at a new weapon that would unleash a "rain of ruin" from the skies.   **July 28**   Japan says it will "ignore" the Potsdam Declaration.

AUGUST

Aug. 6   An atomic bomb is dropped on Hiroshima, killing at least 80,000 civilians.   **Aug. 8**   The USSR declares war on Japan.   **Aug. 9**   A second atomic bomb is dropped on Nagasaki, killing at least 40,000.   **Aug. 9**   The Red Army smashes into Japanese-held Manchuria.   **Aug. 14**   Hirohito tells the Japanese people he has ordered the end of the war and that his people should "bear the unendurable."   **Aug. 15**   Truman names this day V-J Day as millions around the globe celebrate the end of World War II.

SEPTEMBER

Sept. 2   The date is September 1 in the United States and Europe as a Japanese delegation signs surrender papers on the deck of the battleship *Missouri* in Tokyo Bay, signaling the end of World War II.

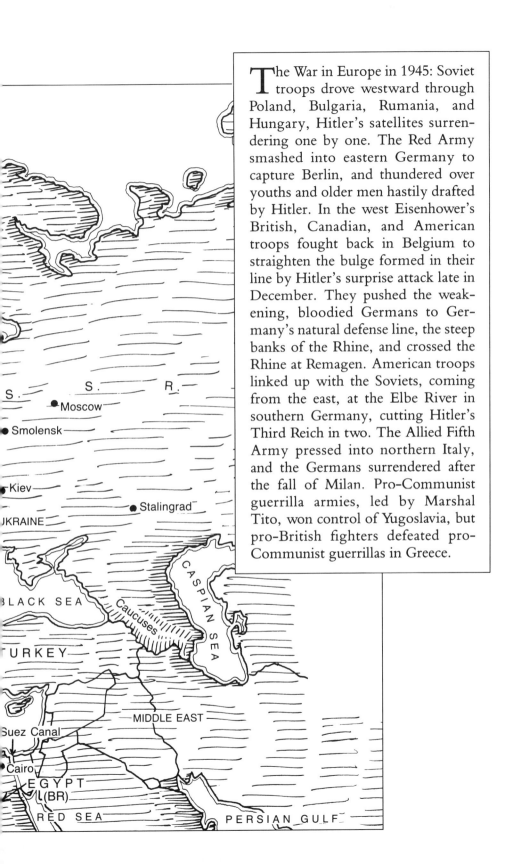

The War in Europe in 1945: Soviet troops drove westward through Poland, Bulgaria, Rumania, and Hungary, Hitler's satellites surrendering one by one. The Red Army smashed into eastern Germany to capture Berlin, and thundered over youths and older men hastily drafted by Hitler. In the west Eisenhower's British, Canadian, and American troops fought back in Belgium to straighten the bulge formed in their line by Hitler's surprise attack late in December. They pushed the weakening, bloodied Germans to Germany's natural defense line, the steep banks of the Rhine, and crossed the Rhine at Remagen. American troops linked up with the Soviets, coming from the east, at the Elbe River in southern Germany, cutting Hitler's Third Reich in two. The Allied Fifth Army pressed into northern Italy, and the Germans surrendered after the fall of Milan. Pro-Communist guerrilla armies, led by Marshal Tito, won control of Yugoslavia, but pro-British fighters defeated pro-Communist guerrillas in Greece.

The War in the Pacific in 1945: Air Force B-29s took off from Guam and Saipan in the Marianas to fire-bomb the cities of Japan. Marines landed and took Iwo Jima after the bloodiest battling in marine history. Soldiers and marines of the Tenth Army captured Okinawa, where American land and sea losses were the heaviest of the Pacific war. General MacArthur's land, sea, and air forces sailed from Leyte in the Philippines to invade the main island of Luzon, first retaking Manila and nearby

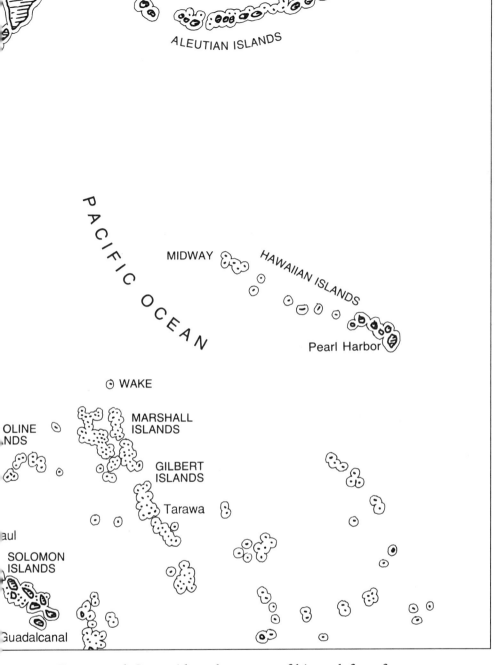

ALEUTIAN ISLANDS

PACIFIC OCEAN

MIDWAY

HAWAIIAN ISLANDS

Pearl Harbor

WAKE

MARSHALL ISLANDS

OLINE NDS

GILBERT ISLANDS

Tarawa

SOLOMON ISLANDS

aul

Guadalcanal

Bataan and Corregidor, the scenes of bitter defeats for MacArthur in 1942. A British-Indian army recaptured Burma and were preparing to attack the Japanese in British Malaya and French Indochina when the war ended. Chinese troops fought off Japanese attacks on American air bases in China. Fighting erupted between Chinese troops led by Nationalist leader Chiang Kai-shek and armies led by Communist leader Mao Tse-tung.

FOR FURTHER READING

All the material, including quotations and dialogue, that appears in the five books of this series has been taken from magazine and newspaper articles, books, and other publications written during and after World War II. For the reader who would like to know more about America's role in that war, I recommend the following books:

Associated Press. *World War II, a 50th Anniversary History*. A Donald Hutter Book. New York: Henry Holt, 1989.

Berry, Henry. *Semper Fi, Mac: Living Memories of U.S. Marines in World War II*. New York: Berkley Publishing, 1982.

Campbell, John. *The Experience of World War II*. New York: Oxford University Press, 1989.

Churchill, Winston. *Memoirs of the Second World War* (an abridgement). Boston: Houghton-Mifflin, 1987.

Devaney, John. *Hitler, Mad Dictator of World War II*. New York: Putnam's, 1978.

———. *Douglas MacArthur, Something of a Hero*. New York: Putnam's, 1979.

———. *Blood and Guts, The Patton Story*. New York: Julian Messner, 1982.

Halsey, William. *Admiral Halsey's Story*. New York: Whittlesey House, 1947.

Manchester, William. *American Caesar: Douglas MacArthur, 1880–1964*. Boston: Little Brown, 1978.

North, John. *Men Fighting—Battle Stories*. London: R. P. Prince, 1948.

Rhodes, Richard. *The Making of the Atomic Bomb*. New York: Simon and Schuster, 1986.

Schmidt, Heinz. *With Rommel in the Desert*. London: G. G. Harrap, 1951.

Shirer, William. *The Rise and Fall of the Third Reich*. New York: Simon and Schuster, 1960.

Sommerville, Donald. *World War II Day by Day*. New York: Dorset Press, 1989.

Sullivan, George. *Strange but True Stories of World War II*. New York: Walker, 1991.

Toland, John. *The Last 100 Days*. New York: Random House, 1965.

Zieser, Benno. *In Their Shallow Graves*. Translated by Alec Browne. London: Elek Books, 1956.

INDEX